Contents

How plants grow

Since the surrounding water provides support, aquatic stems are often much thinner and more flexible than terrestrial stems. Flexible stems allow the plant to move with the water, rather than try to hold steady against it, risking damage. The leaves of terrestrial plants have a thick, waxy outer layer called the cuticle, which protects the plant from drying out. In aquatic plants, this part is much thinner and liquid is able to pass through much more easily, which helps the plant to take up nutrients. Aquatic plants that produce aerial leaves often show two different leaf shapes below and above the water.

Some aquatic plants have clumps, or rosettes, of leaves.

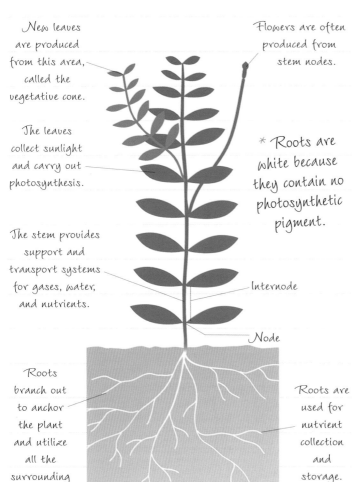

New leaves are produced from this area, called the vegetative cone.

The leaves collect sunlight and carry out photosynthesis.

The stem provides support and transport systems for gases, water, and nutrients.

Flowers are often produced from stem nodes.

* Roots are white because they contain no photosynthetic pigment.

Internode

Node

Roots branch out to anchor the plant and utilize all the surrounding substrate.

Roots are used for nutrient collection and storage.

▲ Large plants produce longer and thicker roots for better anchorage and nutrient collection.

▲ Many plants grow from bulbs or tubers, which contain large reserves of nutrients.

VARIETY OF LEAF SHAPES

The broad variation in leaf shapes reflects their adaptations for survival in different environments. All have photosynthetic pigments, often with a higher concentration on the upper surface, which explains why many leaves have different colors or shades on each side.

▼ *The thin stems and feathery leaves of* Cabomba *are designed for buoyancy.*

▲ *The broad leaves of* Echinodorus *are supported on strong stalks.*

▼ *The fine leaves of hairgrass create a lawn across the tank floor.*

◀ *With upright stems and alternate leaves,* Ludwigia *has the "traditional" growth pattern of many plants.*

How plants grow

Terrestrial plant roots have fine hairs, but these are not present in most aquatic plants, although these hairs may develop on some bog plants when grown out of water. Large plants, such as Echinodorus, produce many long roots to provide good anchorage and a wide nutrient collection area. Smaller plants from shallow or marshy areas have much shorter, thinner roots. In their natural habitats, the substrate is often shallow and there is little water movement, so the plants do not need long roots for anchorage. Some roots are adapted to live above the substrate and will attach themselves to wood and rocks.

Needing no anchorage, floating plants form fine, branched roots.

Anubias produces roots from a rhizome.

▼ Attached to bogwood and rocks, Anubias is adapted to survive above the substrate.

▲ Salvinia has finely branched roots that take up nutrients from the water.

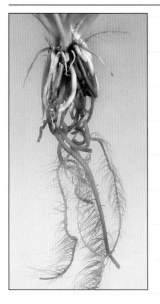

◀ Echinodorus *has thick roots for nutrient storage and fine ones for nutrient collection.*

▼ Cryptocoryne *species are ideally suited to the shallow depths of tropical streams.*

AQUATIC FLOWERS

Most aquatic plants produce seeds and flowers, which grow above water, where they can be pollinated by insects. Some produce flowers beneath the water surface, while a few species do not produce flowers at all.

▼ *Produced on plantlets, the flowers of* Echinodorus *are raised above the plant.*

▲ *Small flowers develop in the leaf axils of* Alternanthera.

How plants grow

Their ability to absorb vital elements directly from the surrounding environment and to obtain energy by photosynthesis has enabled plants to thrive and spread into many habitats, including underwater. A plant has little control over the rate of photosynthesis that occurs within its cells. Several environmental aspects play a vital role, and it is always the component in least supply that becomes the limiting factor. Light is the most obvious environmental component, but temperature, carbon dioxide (CO_2) levels, and nutrient availability all affect the rate of photosynthesis.

HOW PHOTOSYNTHESIS WORKS

Uniquely, plants are able to obtain energy from sunlight, CO_2, and water using the process of photosynthesis.

Pigments such as chlorophyll trap sunlight energy and use it to "power" photosynthesis.

Glucose produced from photosynthesis is stored and used as a food source.

Carbon dioxide supplies the carbon to build carbohydrates.

Water is easily absorbed by aquatic plants.

Oxygen is released as a waste product.

The carbon, oxygen, and hydrogen of CO_2 and water are "rearranged" within the plant cells.

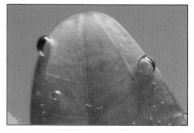

▲ Oxygen produced during photosynthesis is visible on the leaf.

◀ The intensity and duration of light affect the rate of photosynthesis.

THE ONGOING PROCESS OF RESPIRATION

Unlike photosynthesis, respiration is a continual process that does not stop at night. Thus, photosynthesis stores food "energy," whereas respiration releases energy. In any 24-hour period, plants release more oxygen through photosynthesis than they use up during respiration. This is one reason why many fast-growing plants are sold as "oxygenating" plants for ponds and aquariums. However, in addition to plants, fish and bacteria also use up oxygen continually through respiration; in fact, bacteria are the biggest "consumers" of oxygen in the aquarium.

HOW RESPIRATION WORKS

Respiration is the reverse of photosynthesis. It breaks down food sources and releases energy into the cells, using oxygen and producing CO_2 as a waste product.

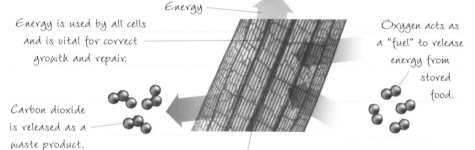

Glucose stored within the plant is broken down to provide energy.

Energy

Energy is used by all cells and is vital for correct growth and repair.

Oxygen acts as a "fuel" to release energy from stored food.

Carbon dioxide is released as a waste product.

Respiration occurs in all plant cells night and day.

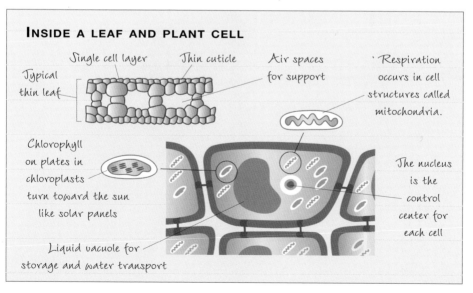

INSIDE A LEAF AND PLANT CELL

Single cell layer   Thin cuticle   Air spaces for support   Respiration occurs in cell structures called mitochondria.

Typical thin leaf

Chlorophyll on plates in chloroplasts turn toward the sun like solar panels

The nucleus is the control center for each cell

Liquid vacuole for storage and water transport

Water quality

The water in which you house living aquatic organisms such as fish and plants is much more than a simple combination of hydrogen and oxygen. Water can be described as hard or soft, and alkaline or acid, and it acts as a carrier for a wealth of minerals, nutrients, toxins, bacteria (both beneficial and harmful), and pollutants. Providing good water quality means ensuring that all these factors are at the correct level so that the water in the aquarium is not only safe for fish and plants but also actively encourages their health and growth.

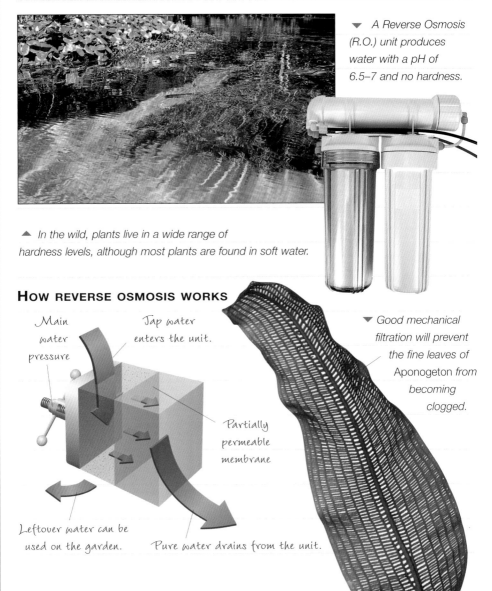

▼ *A Reverse Osmosis (R.O.) unit produces water with a pH of 6.5–7 and no hardness.*

▲ *In the wild, plants live in a wide range of hardness levels, although most plants are found in soft water.*

HOW REVERSE OSMOSIS WORKS

Main water pressure

Tap water enters the unit.

Partially permeable membrane

Leftover water can be used on the garden.

Pure water drains from the unit.

▼ *Good mechanical filtration will prevent the fine leaves of Aponogeton from becoming clogged.*

▼ Tap water from hard water areas has high levels of mineral salts.

▼ Rainwater is a good source of almost pure water, with slight acidity and no hardness.

◀ Treat tap water with a dechlorinator to remove chlorine, chloramines, and heavy metals.

CREATING SOFT WATER

For soft water, mix R.O. or filtered rainwater with dechlorinated tap water. Add a pH buffer to retain stability.

CREATING HARD WATER

Use calcium-based substrates and rockwork with dechlorinated tap water. Also use calcium-based trace element additives.

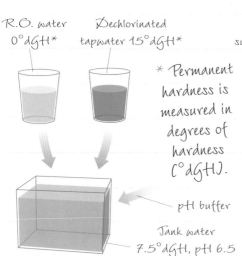

R.O. water 0°dGH*   Dechlorinated tapwater 15°dGH*

* Permanent hardness is measured in degrees of hardness (°dGH).

pH buffer

Jank water 7.5°dGH, pH 6.5

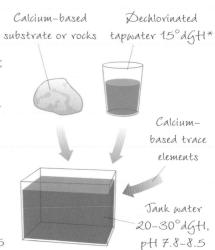

Calcium-based substrate or rocks   Dechlorinated tapwater 15°dGH*

Calcium-based trace elements

Jank water 20–30°dGH, pH 7.8–8.5

Water quality

Controlling the levels of nitrogen-containing compounds in the water is a vital aspect of good fish keeping. Plants use nitrates as a food source but, like fish, are poisoned by ammonia.

THE NITROGEN CYCLE

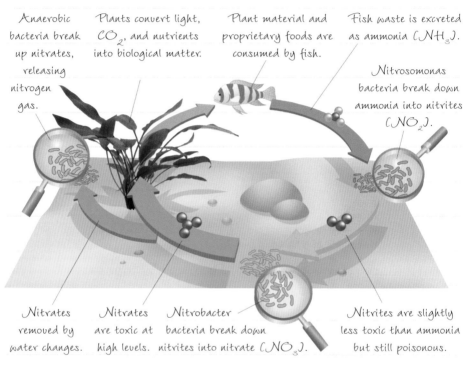

Anaerobic bacteria break up nitrates, releasing nitrogen gas.

Plants convert light, CO_2, and nutrients into biological matter.

Plant material and proprietary foods are consumed by fish.

Fish waste is excreted as ammonia (NH_3).

Nitrosomonas bacteria break down ammonia into nitrites (NO_2).

Nitrates removed by water changes.

Nitrates are toxic at high levels.

Nitrobacter bacteria break down nitrites into nitrate (NO_3).

Nitrites are slightly less toxic than ammonia but still poisonous.

AQUARIUM FILTRATION

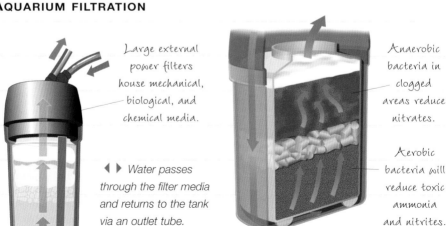

Large external power filters house mechanical, biological, and chemical media.

◀ ▶ *Water passes through the filter media and returns to the tank via an outlet tube.*

Anaerobic bacteria in clogged areas reduce nitrates.

Aerobic bacteria will reduce toxic ammonia and nitrites.

TESTING pH AND HARDNESS

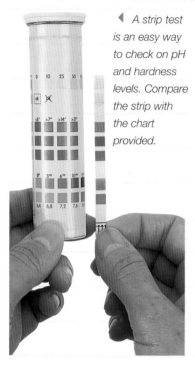

◄ *A strip test is an easy way to check on pH and hardness levels. Compare the strip with the chart provided.*

HOW pH WORKS

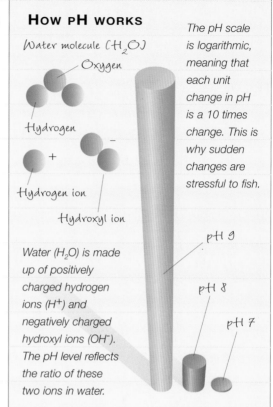

Water molecule (H₂O)

Oxygen

Hydrogen

Hydrogen ion +

Hydroxyl ion −

pH 9

pH 8

pH 7

The pH scale is logarithmic, meaning that each unit change in pH is a 10 times change. This is why sudden changes are stressful to fish.

Water (H₂O) is made up of positively charged hydrogen ions (H⁺) and negatively charged hydroxyl ions (OH⁻). The pH level reflects the ratio of these two ions in water.

USING LIQUID TESTS

▼ *Add the specified number of equal drops of one or more reagents to a water sample.*

▲ *This broad range pH test shows a value of 8.5—alkaline water.*

▼ *This nitrite test shows a reading of 0.1mg/liter. Ideally, it should be 0.*

▲ *In a planted aquarium with fish, aim for 0 nitrate.*

Using substrates

In the rivers and streams in which many aquatic plants grow, the substrates vary depending on the environmental and geological conditions of the river system and the local area. Aquatic plants are often found in sandy, muddy, or gravel beds. The dense muddy substrate found in many places provides an ideal anchoring medium that holds plants firmly in position. In natural conditions, the roots may grow far wider and deeper than they possibly could in an aquarium. In an average aquarium, the substrate is likely to be a fairly straightforward affair, usually a simple covering of pea gravel. Plants use the substrate not only as a place to root but also as a source of nutrients and, in some cases, a medium through which to reproduce.

▼ Mixing black quartz and pebbles with fine gravel creates a substrate with texture.

▲ Using pebbles of various sizes gives a natural feel to the aquarium substrate.

* A substrate made up of particles that are too large will allow water to pass through easily, removing nutrients.

◀ Used with care, sterilized potting mix can make an excellent planting medium.

▶ In this calm and slow-flowing waterway, sediment is deposited and then builds up on top of a rocky bed. Toward the edges, the sediment is deep and provides an ideal substrate for plants to root.

USING SUBSTRATES

POPULAR AQUARIUM SUBSTRATES

Sand is the best medium to cover a heating cable.

Laterite-based substrate provides long-term nutrients.

Lime-free substrate is inert and ideal for supporting roots.

Pea gravel is best used as a top layer in planted aquariums.

▶ Sand makes an interesting and attractive substrate for an aquarium display, but it requires regular maintenance to prevent compaction and stagnation.

◀ Provide a layer of substrate up to 4 inches (10 centemeters) deep for plant roots to grow into.

▲ Wash gravel thoroughly to remove dust that will cloud the water.

Using substrates

The substrate is slightly warmer than the main body of water in natural rivers and streams. The currents produced as a result of the temperature differences help to move nutrients around the plant roots. Similar currents can be created in the aquarium using a substrate heating cable. Placed on the base, it produces a very gentle heat that raises the temperature of the surrounding substrate. A heating cable does not need a thermostat and can be left on continuously—heat output and power consumption are low.

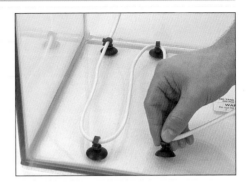

1 Attach the substrate heating cable to the base of the tank with suckers, leaving a 2–4 in (5–10 cm) space between the loops.

2 Add 2 in (5 cm) of silver sand to cover the cable by 0.4–0.8 in (1–2 cm). Next, add a thin layer of nutrient-rich substrate.

3 Finally, add a 2–4 in (5–10 cm)–deep layer of lime-free substrate. Lime-free gravel is a good, inert rooting medium.

Lime-free gravel

Nutrient rich substrate

Sand distributes heat evenly

Heating cable

AEROBIC AND ANAEROBIC CONDITIONS

A substrate rich in organic material (waste matter and nutrient-rich substrates) contains large numbers of bacteria that break down these organics into usable nutrients. Most bacteria quickly use up oxygen, with the result that the substrate becomes anaerobic. In anaerobic conditions, different types of bacteria form, which do not need large quantities of oxygen or can create their own. These anaerobic bacteria can release toxic gases, most notably hydrogen sulphide, which can cause plant roots to rot, damage fish health and encourage algae. However, anaerobic conditions also allow nutrients to become more readily available to plants by preventing the binding of nutrients with oxygen molecules. As the bacteria use up the nitrates, nitrogen is released—another important nutrient. A mixture of aerobic and anaerobic substrate zones can provide the benefits of both conditions. A low-oxygen substrate is often best, where anaerobic conditions are allowed to develop in some places, but not in others.

USING SUBSTRATES

Hydrogen sulphide is produced by bacterial breakdown of organic material.

Oxygen is taken in (as well as produced during photosynthesis) by plant leaves and transported down to the root system.

Nitrogen gas is released by the action of denitrifying bacteria, which obtain oxygen from nitrites and nitrates.

Plants extend their roots into both aerobic and anaerobic substrate.

At the surface, the substrate is aerobic due to close contact with the oxygen-containing aquarium water.

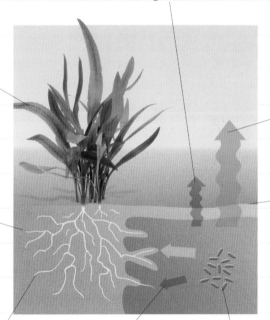

Oxygen released by plant roots keeps the substrate around the root aerobic.

Toxic substances can damage plant roots.

Bacteria in the anaerobic area break down nutrient bonds, allowing nutrients to be easily assimilated by plants.

Choosing plants

Choosing different plants and estimating the quantities required takes careful thought and planning. The overall display should be the result of a buildup of plants that gradually become established. They need not all be introduced at the same time; indeed, there are advantages to taking a "staggered" approach. Introduce the slow-establishing plants (including many foreground and harder-to-keep species) before fast-growing and fast-establishing species. It is always worth introducing a number of different species to see which do better than others.

𝒫lenty of air in the bags provides cushioning and prevents damage in transit.

▼ *Finding a good source of healthy plants is vital. Tanks should be well-lit, clean, and tidy.*

▲ *Mail-order plants should arrive with the plants in plastic sleeves and separated in trays.*

* It is worth buying more than you need when obtaining mail-order plants to compensate for any losses.

CHOOSING A HEALTHY PLANT

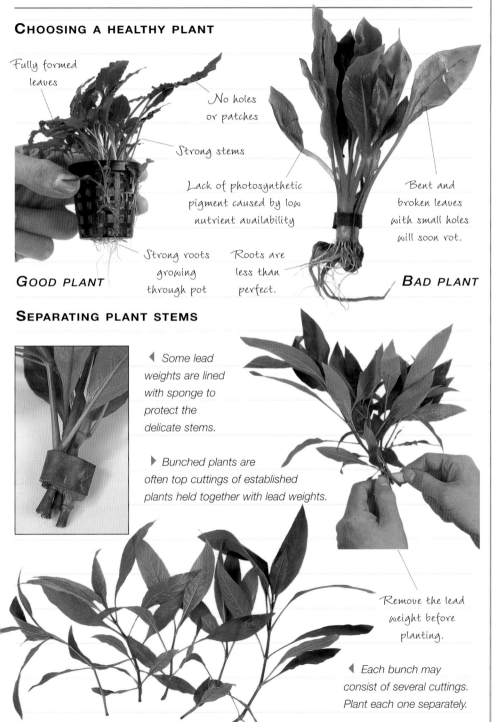

Fully formed leaves

No holes or patches

Strong stems

Lack of photosynthetic pigment caused by low nutrient availability

Strong roots growing through pot

Roots are less than perfect.

Bent and broken leaves with small holes will soon rot.

GOOD PLANT

BAD PLANT

SEPARATING PLANT STEMS

◀ Some lead weights are lined with sponge to protect the delicate stems.

▶ Bunched plants are often top cuttings of established plants held together with lead weights.

Remove the lead weight before planting.

◀ Each bunch may consist of several cuttings. Plant each one separately.

Planting techniques

There are a few points to bear in mind before you put any plants into the aquarium. First, the substrate and decor (rocks, wood, etc.) should be in place, as well as the filtration, lighting, and heating equipment. Secondly, although most plants should be snail-free, you should examine the leaves and stems thoroughly for both snails and snail eggs. Make sure the roots are healthy, and remove any damaged leaves and stems, as these are unlikely to recover. Removing the leaves should encourage new growth.

Planting *Vallisneria*

* The straplike leaves of Vallisneria create height at the back of the aquarium.

1 Remove the lead weight before planting. Do not be tempted to plant these slim leaves in one clump.

Check plants for damage.

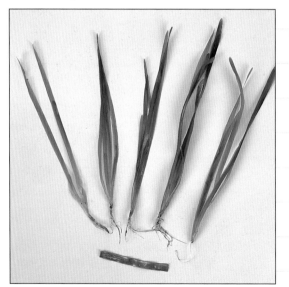

2 Each cutting has a healthy root system. Plant them individually, leaving space for growth.

3 Make a hole in the substrate and slide in the plant just deep enough to prevent it from coming loose.

PLANTING TECHNIQUES

PLANTING *LUDWIGIA*

2 Create a dip in the substrate with your fingers and hold it open.

3 Put in the plant and cover the roots with substrate. Firm the soil gently.

4 Put in plants 1–2 in (2.5–5 cm) apart or leave room so that the tips of the leaves on separate plants just touch.

1 Slide the plants, embedded in rockwool, out of the pot. Carefully unravel the rockwool. There may be as many as three plants in each piece.

PLANTING *ECHINODORUS*

2 Remove any leaves that show signs of damage by gently pulling the "stem" from the base.

3 Gently place the roots into the substrate, taking care to cover the white area at the base of the plant.

1 Ease the plant from its pot. Trim away any long roots to reduce damage during planting. The plant will soon produce new ones.

Long roots are difficult to plant.

Planting techniques

When putting in the first aquatic plants, leave space between them for growth and propagation. Most stem plants should be planted at least 2–4 in (5–10 cm) apart to allow room for the leaves to grow without blocking out light to the foliage of their neighbors. This will also give you space to plant top cuttings at some future date if you wish. Many foreground plants reproduce by means of runners. Allowing existing plants to grow and spread naturally often creates a more realistic effect than filling the foreground area with new plants. A few common aquatic plants are better suited for planting on porous rocks or wood, rather than in the substrate. Typical examples include *Anubias, Microsorium* (Java fern), *Vesicularia* (Java moss), and *Bolbitis* species.

PLANTING *CABOMBA*

1 Remove the lead weight and separate the cuttings. Take care, as *Cabomba* is a delicate plant that bruises easily and may rot at the base.

2 Using a pair of sharp scissors, cut away the bare stem just below a leaf joint. For shorter pieces, cut further up the stem.

* *Once prepared for planting, lay all plants out on a tray in shallow water to prevent them from drying out.*

3 Put in each plant individually. Start planting at the rear of the aquarium and work carefully toward the front.

ATTACHING JAVA FERN TO BOGWOOD

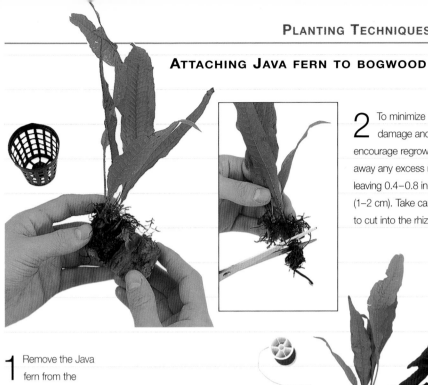

2 To minimize damage and encourage regrowth, trim away any excess root, leaving 0.4–0.8 in (1–2 cm). Take care not to cut into the rhizome.

1 Remove the Java fern from the rockwool. This can be tricky, as the roots are often dense and tangled.

Specimens with healthy leaves will grow away more quickly.

3 Set the plant on the wood in a natural position and tie the roots to the bogwood with black cotton. It will soon be covered by the new roots and hardly visible.

▲ *This* Anubias *has established well on bogwood. It will grow through the water surface.*

Lighting for plants

Providing a suitable light source, combined with good environmental conditions, will ensure that aquarium plants are able to photosynthesize at an optimum rate and remain healthy. To provide the correct light source, it is important to understand how plants use light in nature and what qualities light possesses.

THE INGREDIENTS OF LIGHT

White light is made up of different wavelengths, each corresponding to a specific color. Plants use only some of the light they receive, concentrating on specific areas of the spectrum and using only certain wavelengths, usually those that are most readily available. Chlorophyll uses mostly blue and red light.

▲ Splitting white light through a prism shows the spectrum of colours.

Sunlight peaks in the blue area of the spectrum. Blue is used by plants and algae.

Green light is reflected by the majority of plants.

Aquatic plants' photosynthetic ability is most sensitive to red light between 650 and 680nm*.

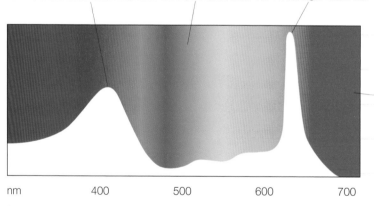

Light in the infrared area (700–750nm) cannot be used by plants*.

| nm | 400 | 500 | 600 | 700 |

WHY ARE PLANTS GREEN?

Most plants appear green because the light-absorbing pigment, chlorophyll, absorbs red and blue light but does not use the green part of the spectrum—it simply reflects it, thus producing a green appearance.

* Wavelengths of light are measured in nanometers (nm) — billionths of a meter.

▲ *In some areas of the Amazon River, the water is crystal clear, and the sunlit shallows are brimming with aquatic plants of all kinds.*

ZONES OF LIGHT AND PLANT GROWTH

PLANTS FOR LOW LIGHT

The plants in this group are ideal for aquariums with just one or two fluorescent tubes. Some will live happily in a wide range of lighting conditions; others prefer to be in shaded areas or away from bright light. Use bogwood or rocks to create shady zones in the tank.

Anubias barteri var. *barteri*
Anubias barteri var. *nana*
Anubias congensis
Anubias lanceolata
Aponogeton elongatus
Aponogeton madagascariensis
Cryptocoryne affinis
Cryptocoryne lutea
Cryptocoryne walkeri
Lemna minor
Microsorium pteropus
Spathiphyllum wallisii
Vesicularia dubyana

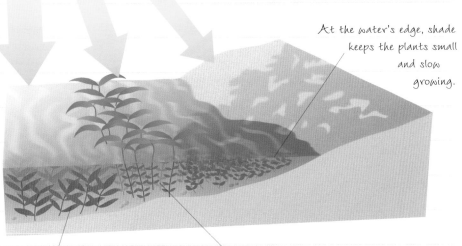

At the water's edge, shade keeps the plants small and slow growing.

In the center, plants receive plenty of light but must bend with the currents.

In open areas of deeper water, thick-stemmed plants thrive in the bright light.

Lighting for plants

Fluorescent tubes are an efficient and relatively cheap way of lighting smaller planted tanks. By altering the coating on the inside of the tube, the spectrum of light emitted can be changed, so fluorescent tubes can be designed for specific purposes and to emit specific colors.

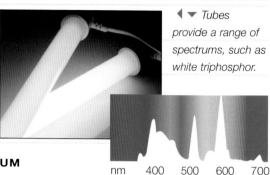

◀ ▼ *Tubes provide a range of spectrums, such as white triphosphor.*

nm   400   500   600   700

LIGHT LOSS IN THE AQUARIUM

Light from a fluorescent tube is emitted in all directions.

Condensation trays must be kept clean to reduce light absorption.

Some light is refracted from the water surface.

Suspended particles soak up a great deal of light.

Light is lost through the tank glass.

Bottom plants receive only a small part of the emitted light.

Reflectors help to redirect light into the aquarium.

As the light passes through the water, its spectrum is altered and intensity reduced as it is absorbed and converted into heat energy.

Large-leaved and tall plants take up light and reduce the amount reaching smaller and lower plants.

PLANTS FOR MODERATE LIGHT

These plants can be kept with two or three fluorescent tubes and are relatively hardy species. Although some will survive and grow under only one or two tubes (with reflectors to maximize the levels of light actually reaching the plants), they will not grow at an optimum rate and may not show their full health. Most of the plants in this group will do better with brighter light, but they do not require it.

Anubias angustifolia "Afzelii"
Anubias gracilis
Azolla caroliniana
Azolla filiculoides
Ceratophyllum demersum
Crinum thaianum
Cryptocoryne balansae
Cryptocoryne cordata
Cryptocoryne pontederiifolia
Echinodorus cordifolius
Echinodorus macrophyllus
Egeria densa
Vallisneria spiralis

DIFFERENT LIGHTING EFFECTS

◀ A "pink" tube used on its own creates a strange hue and is best mixed with a white light.

◀ A white full-spectrum tube creates a realistic and well-balanced lighting effect.

◀ Spotlights provide pools of high-intensity light that are good for plant growth and that form a dramatic tank display.

▶ Fluorescent tubes emit light in all directions. Using a reflector can redirect light into the tank and significantly improve light intensity for the plants. These reflectors are made of mirror-finish plastic or aluminium.

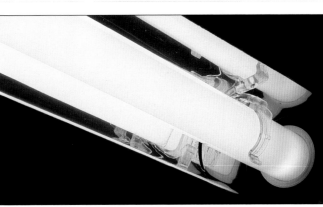

LIGHTING FOR PLANTS

Lighting for plants

Many aquarium plants originate from tropical regions, generally near the banks of medium to large rivers where the water is shallower and the plants can obtain light more easily. Plants that are accustomed to open environments will require strong lighting for longer periods, while plants found in the shade of vegetation will require a less-intense light source. It is important that plants in the aquarium receive the right level and duration of light to reflect their natural origins. They must also receive periods of darkness.

SIESTA TIME FOR PLANTS

A good method of reducing or controlling algae growth in the aquarium is to provide a midday "siesta" period. A 5–6 hour period of lighting, followed by 2–3 hours of no artificial light and then another 5–6 hours of lighting proves effective at reducing algae growth without any adverse effects on fish or plants in the aquarium. Timer switches can be used to achieve this.

LIGHT IN NATURE

In tropical regions, plants receive about 10–12 hours of strong light per day.

The most intense light is in the middle part of day.

Gradual transition at dawn and dusk.

0   2   4   6   8   10   12   14   16   18   20   22   24

LIGHT IN THE AQUARIUM

Timer switches stagger lights.

Pattern of aquarium lighting should be similar to natural light.

Siesta slows algae growth.

0   2   4   6   8   10   12   14   16   18   20   22   24

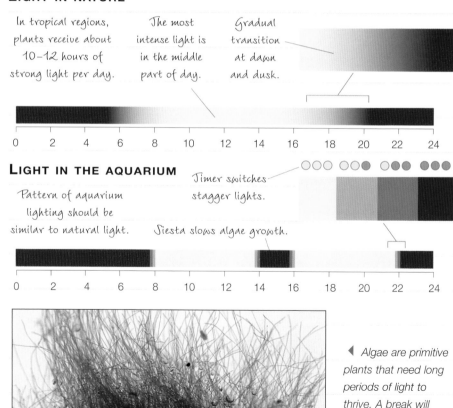

◀ *Algae are primitive plants that need long periods of light to thrive. A break will reduce their growth.*

PLANTS FOR BRIGHT LIGHT

If the plants are densely grouped together, use metal-halide (halogen) or mercury vapor lamps; if they are not and there is plenty of open space, then fluorescent tubes will be adequate.

Alternanthera reineckii
Anubias gracilis
Aponogeton boivinianus
Aponogeton crispus
Aponogeton ulvaceus
Aponogeton undulatus
Bacopa caroliniana
Bacopa monnieri
Bacopa rotundifolia
Barclaya longifolia

Bolbitis heudelotii
Cabomba caroliniana
Cardamine lyrata
Ceratophyllum submersum
Ceratopteris cornuta
Crassula helmsii
Crinum natans
Crinum thaianum
Cryptocoryne albida
Cryptocoryne balansae
Cryptocoryne beckettii
Cryptocoryne ciliata
Cryptocoryne moehlmannii
Cryptocoryne siamensis
Cryptocoryne undulata
Cryptocoryne wendtii
Cryptocoryne willisii
Echinodorus amazonicus
Echinodorus bleheri
Echinodorus bolivianus
Echinodorus grandiflorus
Echinodorus horemanii
Echinodorus major
Echinodorus opacus
Echinodorus osiris
Echinodorus parviflorus

Echinodorus tenellus
Echinodorus uruguayensis
Eichhornia crassipes
Eleocharis acicularis
Eleocharis vivipara
Elodea canadensis
Gymnocoronis
   spilanthoides
Hemianthus callitrichoides
Hemianthus
   micranthemoides
Hydrocotyle leucocephala
Hygrophila corymbosa
Hygrophila polysperma
Lagarosiphon major
Limnobium laevigatum
Lobelia cardinalis
Ludwigia helminthorrhiza
Ludwigia repens
Marsilea hirsuta
Najas indica
Nuphar japonica
Nymphaea lotus
Pistia stratiotes
Potamogeton mascarensis
Riccia fluitans
Rotala rotundifolia
Sagittaria platyphylla
Sagittaria pusilla
Sagittaria subulata
Salvinia auriculata
Salvinia minima
Salvinia natans
Salvinia oblongifolia
Samolus valerandi
Saururus cernuus
Vallisneria (most species)

Lighting for plants

For larger and deeper planted aquariums, brighter sources of light such as metal-halide or mercury vapor lamps may be required. Both of these types of lamps are suspended above the aquarium rather than being fitted within a closed hood. Metal-halide lamps provide an intense, high-output light via a tungsten filament. Although they are expensive, they provide the best output for demanding aquarium plants. Mercury vapor lamps provide a much higher output than fluorescent tubes and are relatively low cost to run. At first glance, using natural sunlight to illuminate aquarium plants seems an ideal solution, but getting the balance right and preventing unwanted algal growth make this strategy the least attractive.

▼ *Common in marine tanks, a mix of metal-halide and fluorescent tubes produce bright, balanced light.*

USEFUL DEFINITIONS

Lumen: Unit of luminous energy, historically the light from one candle.

Lux: Unit of illumination representing 1 lumen falling on 1 square meter.

Watt: Unit of electrical power.

* Some plants may be harmed by a sudden change to bright light— alter levels gradually.

▶ *This lighting unit houses a single metal-halide lamp that provides an intense level of light suitable for deeper planted aquariums.*

◀ *Mercury vapor lamps produce a high output and look attractive over open tanks.*

▲ *Red plants, such as this* Myriophyllum, *thrive in very bright light conditions.*

PLANTS FOR BRIGHT TO VERY BRIGHT LIGHT

These plants require a high-intensity light for a large proportion of daylight hours. In most cases, fluorescent tubes will not provide sufficient light to promote good growth. Use metal-halide or mercury vapor lamps.

Alternanthera reineckii
Ammannia gracilis
Bacopa monnieri
Blyxa echinosperma
Blyxa japonica
Cabomba aquatica
Cabomba piauhyensis
Cryptocoryne parva
Didiplis diandra
Echinodorus macrophyllus

Eichhornia azurea
Eichhornia crassipes
Eleocharis parvula
Eusteralis stellata
Fontinalis antipyretica
Glossostigma elatinoides
Heteranthera zosterifolia
Hydrocotyle sibthorpioides
Hydrocotyle verticillata
Hygrophila corymbosa
   "Crispa"
Hygrophila corymbosa
   "Strigosa"
Hygrophila difformis
Hygrophila guianensis
Hygrophila stricta
Lilaeopsis novae-zelandiae
Limnophila aquatica
Limnophila indica
Limnophila sessiliflora

Ludwigia brevipes
Ludwigia glandulosa
Ludwigia palustris
   (any variety)
Lysimachia nummularia
Micranthemum umbrosum
Myriophyllum aquaticum
Myriophyllum hippuroides
Myriophyllum scabratum
Myriophyllum tuberculatum
Nesaea crassicaulis
Nymphaea lotus var. rubra
Nymphaea stellata
Nymphoides aquatica
Potamogeton crispus
Potamogeton gayii
Rotala macrandra
Rotala wallichii
Shinnersia rivularis
Trapa natans

FEEDING PLANTS

Feeding plants

If they are to grow properly and remain healthy, aquarium plants require carbon dioxide to "fuel" the process of photosynthesis and a number of minerals and organic nutrients, which they take in through either their leaves or roots. Supplying the correct fertilizers is like giving your plants a balanced diet. The quantity and type of fertilizers you supply depends on the number of fish and plants in the aquarium, lighting, and water temperature. Waste matter produced by fish is used by plants as a source of food, so a well-stocked aquarium needs less additional fertilizer. In a well-lit tank with high temperatures, plants grow quickly and need more nutrients.

▲ *The correct dosage is vital when using liquid fertilization.*

NUTRIENT FLOW IN NATURE

Water rises by convection as it is warmed by the substrate.

Heat from the sun warms the substrate.

Some nutrients are absorbed directly through the leaves.

Plant roots absorb nutrients from the substrate.

The substrate is slightly warmer than the water above it.

Water circulation carries nutrients down to the substrate.

▲ *Tablet fertilizers release nutrients into the area immediately surrounding the plant.*

HOW CHELATES HELP FEEDING

Nutrient molecules bound with oxygen become too large to pass into the plant.

Nutrients bind with chelates in the substrate to help absorption.

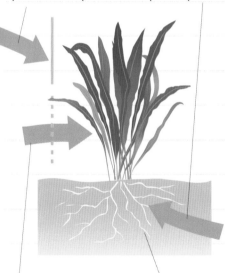

Liquid fertilizers with chelates make nutrients small enough to be absorbed.

Roots release chemicals that help the plant absorb nutrients.

FERTILIZING AQUARIUM PLANTS ACCURATELY

A few simple tips should help you to fertilize your aquarium plants accurately.

A turbulent water surface will reduce the amount of CO_2 the aquarium can hold. Ensure that the filter outflow is at least 4 in (10 cm) below the water surface. Avoid any unnecessary aeration.

If you are using tap water and a nutrient-rich (slow-release) substrate, you may not need to use a liquid fertilizer. Tap water often contains many of the key nutrients that plants require. Rainwater and R.O. water are virtually devoid of nutrients, so liquid fertilizer is a must.

Only add fertilizers specifically designed for aquarium use. Terrestrial plant fertilizers contain excess nitrates and chemicals that may be harmful to fish and aquatic plants.

Never use adsorbent filter media, such as activated carbon, unless for a specific (short-term) reason, as these will remove useful nutrients.

Regardless of nitrate levels, carry out regular small water changes to remove and replenish nutrients.

It is always better to introduce regular, small doses of fertilizers than irregular or infrequent large doses.

FEEDING PLANTS

Feeding plants

Fertilizers provide plants with substances that are not always available in sufficient quantities from the aquarium water. If a plant becomes unhealthy due to a lack or excess of one or more of these substances, nutritional problems result. Of all the nutrients essential for good plant growth, iron is the most important and is used in the most abundance by plants. In some cases, an excess of one nutrient can create a deficiency in another.

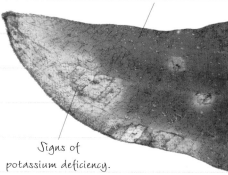

Algae on a young leaf indicates a lack of growth.

SIGNS OF NUTRIENT DEFICIENCY

Signs of potassium deficiency.

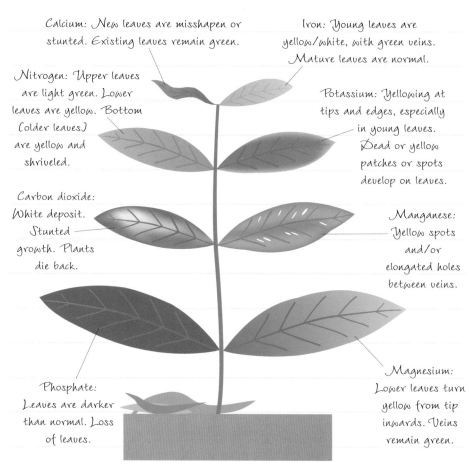

Calcium: New leaves are misshapen or stunted. Existing leaves remain green.

Iron: Young leaves are yellow/white, with green veins. Mature leaves are normal.

Nitrogen: Upper leaves are light green. Lower leaves are yellow. Bottom (older leaves) are yellow and shriveled.

Potassium: Yellowing at tips and edges, especially in young leaves. Dead or yellow patches or spots develop on leaves.

Carbon dioxide: White deposit. Stunted growth. Plants die back.

Manganese: Yellow spots and/or elongated holes between veins.

Phosphate: Leaves are darker than normal. Loss of leaves.

Magnesium: Lower leaves turn yellow from tip inwards. Veins remain green.

NUTRIENT-RICH SUBSTRATES

Clay-based substrates, often called laterite, are available that contain a multitude of nutrients and trace elements vital to plant health. Most of these are soil-like in appearance and must be "sandwiched" between two layers of substrate that hold the nutrient-rich medium in place. If allowed to escape, some of the laterite may float and muddy the water. You only need a thin spread of this additive to provide significant benefits for the plants.

1 Sprinkle the laterite evenly over the top two-thirds of the gravel substrate in the tank.

2 Gently mix small amounts of a bacterial culture that will help plants use the nutrients.

3 Smooth out the gravel to ensure that the laterite is evenly mixed with the substrate.

4 Add the remaining one-third of gravel. The depth should be 3–4 in (7.5–10 cm).

INTRODUCING CO₂ GAS

Plastic tube carries CO_2 gas into the tank.

Gentle streams of gas bubbles flow into the water.

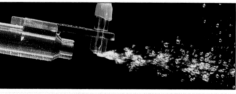

▲ Bubbles of CO_2 gas from the nozzle are circulated by the water pump.

▶ A plastic fermentation container, water pump, some yeast, and tubing make up this CO_2 kit.

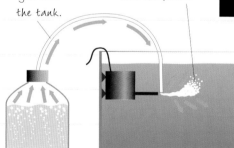

Yeast and sugar solution produce CO_2 gas.

Small electric water pump creates water flow to distribute CO_2 gas.

Propagating plants

In a healthy aquarium environment, many common aquarium plants will propagate themselves without any intervention from the aquarist. Other plants, often those with central stems, can be propagated by a number of artificial methods.

SEXUAL PROPAGATION

In the wild, many aquatic plants reproduce sexually by producing flowers and seeds, or spores. Sexual propagation requires two or more plants to produce flowers above the water surface, but this is difficult to control in the aquarium. Once flowers are produced they must be pollinated. To carry out the process artificially, transfer pollen from the stamen (male) to the stigmas (female) using a fine brush. If pollination is successful and seeds are produced, plant them quickly as they do not last long before starting to germinate.

Spathiphyllum wallisii produces flowers and seeds that can be planted in damp soil.

▲ Pistia stratiotes *produces new plants on runners that break apart, leaving a fully formed plant.*

◀ Spathiphyllum wallisii *is robust enough to survive above and below water.*

* *Most aquatic plants reproduce asexually, meaning the parent plant produces genetically identical "daughter" plants.*

PROPAGATING FROM SEED

Sprinkle the delicate seeds onto damp soil.

As the seeds begin to sprout, add a little water, just covering the leaves.

As the plants grow, keep raising the water level. At 4 in (10 cm), move the seedlings into the aquarium.

PROPAGATING FROM A RUNNER

Daughter plants ready for planting

The mother plant may produce several runners.

◀ *Many aquatic plants produce runners. This is an* Echinodorus.

1 Once each daughter plant has at least two or three leaves, cut off the runner with sharp scissors.

2 Separate the individual plants, leaving a small length of runner on each side.

3 Put each plant into the substrate, leaving a 2 in (5 cm) gap for future growth.

PROPAGATING PLANTS

Propagating plants

Propagation is a good way of increasing the number of plants in the aquarium, as well as replacing old or tattered ones. Aquatic plants reproduce naturally by means of runners, offsets, and adventitious plantlets that are easy to separate from the parent plant and relocate.

ADVENTITIOUS PLANTLETS

Small plants may form on the leaves, stem nodes, or shoots of an adult plant, depending on species. Once they have reached a good size, they can be removed and replanted.

▶ *New plantlets with well-developed roots are visible at the tip of this Java fern leaf.*

1 The mother leaf is beginning to die back to allow the plantlets to drop off. This makes them easier to remove by hand.

2 Pull the plantlet away from the main leaf. As the mother leaf is falling apart, remove and discard it, otherwise it will simply rot away.

▶ *One leaf may produce several plantlets. Check how many individual plants there are. Even quite small plantlets can be carefully separated and replanted.*

▶ *A new shoot to the right of the rhizome of this African fern* (Bolbitis heudelotii) *indicates that this is the growing end and the best area from which to take a cutting.*

PROPAGATING FROM CUTTINGS

1 To take a top cutting, snip off a length of stem with several leaves or nodes. Take cuttings from the fastest-growing stem.

2 Strip away the leaves from one or two nodes to encourage rooting.

* *Virtually all stem plants can be propagated by cuttings taken from both the top and middle stem areas.*

3 Push the cutting into the substrate so that the lower leaves are just resting on the surface. The plant will establish quickly, although the lower leaves may die off.

PROPAGATING PLANTS

PROPAGATING PLANTS

Propagating plants

Plants that grow in clumps will either produce offsets or carry on producing leaves from the main rootstock. If a plant is large enough, you can divide the main root, creating two or more separate plants. Depending on the condition of the rootstock, either pull the plant apart gently or cut it with a sharp knife. Plant the divisions separately. In the case of plants with a rhizome, remove the whole plant from the substrate and cut it into sections. Each piece should have at least one good shoot. Trim the excess roots before replanting them into the substrate.

DIVIDING *CRYPTOCORYNE*

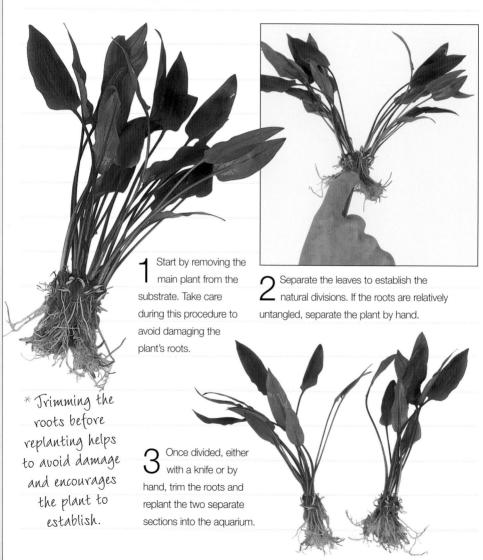

1 Start by removing the main plant from the substrate. Take care during this procedure to avoid damaging the plant's roots.

2 Separate the leaves to establish the natural divisions. If the roots are relatively untangled, separate the plant by hand.

* *Trimming the roots before replanting helps to avoid damage and encourages the plant to establish.*

3 Once divided, either with a knife or by hand, trim the roots and replant the two separate sections into the aquarium.

DIVIDING JAVA FERN

* *Because Java fern grows above the substrate, the rhizome is easy to see.*

▼ *A good specimen can be divided into a number of plants.*

Scissors or knives should always be sharp.

▶ *This Java fern can be left to spread across the wood or divided into two, with one half replanted elsewhere in the aquarium. The divisions should start to grow very soon.*

Keeping plants healthy

If left unattended, a planted aquarium can quickly become a tangled mess of vegetation. As well as checking for damage and disease, also spend time at least once a week on your plants, removing dead leaves and debris to ensure that the display remains at its best.

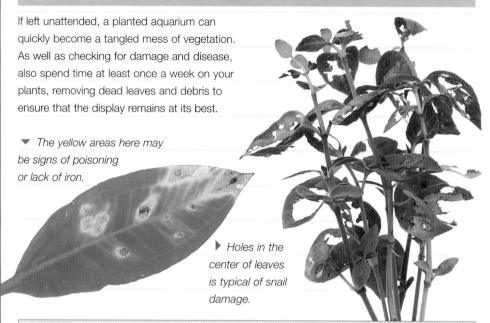

▼ The yellow areas here may be signs of poisoning or lack of iron.

▶ Holes in the center of leaves is typical of snail damage.

SNAILS IN THE AQUARIUM

Whether or not snails are damaging in the aquarium depends on the number present. Snails can enter the aquarium environment via a number of routes, most commonly via live plants. Most live plants now available are relatively snail-free, but it is always best to check them thoroughly first. It is possible to dip aquarium plants in a proprietary chemical before introducing them into the aquarium to kill any snails. Avoid plants from ponds or any other outside source; you risk introducing not only snails but also other pests and aquatic diseases.

If snails are an existing problem, remove them by hand and control their breeding by reducing the amount of organic waste in the tank by regular gravel cleaning. You can also keep snail-eating fish, such as clown loaches. Use proprietary snail killers with extreme caution—they may be based on metals dangerous to some delicate fish and will adversely affect and even kill some plants.

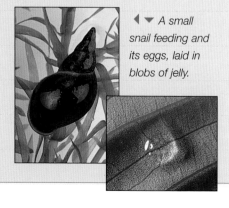

◀ ▼ A small snail feeding and its eggs, laid in blobs of jelly.

PREVENTING ALGAE IN THE AQUARIUM

There are a few steps you can take to avoid a proliferation of unwanted algae. Provided these are followed and plant feeding is not excessive, algae should be easy to control. It is quite common to experience small algal blooms in a new aquarium, although these should go away within a few weeks.

Introduce a group of small algae-eaters, such as *Otocinclus* spp. and/or loaches and suckermouth catfish. Stick to smaller species to avoid disruption.

Avoid direct sunlight at all costs; even the best-kept aquarium will succumb to algal blooms if placed in direct sunlight.

▲ *Dwarf* Otocinclus *eats algae.*

Make sure the aquarium receives no more than 12 hours of artificial lighting per day. If possible, introduce a midday siesta period (see page 28).

Be sure to use the correct spectrum and intensity of lighting units in the aquarium.

Clean the gravel regularly using a gravel siphon to reduce the buildup of organic material.

Carry out regular small water changes to reduce the buildup of nitrates and phosphates in the aquarium.

Avoid overdosing the water with liquid nutrients, and do not use fertilizers containing phosphates.

ARE FISH EATING MY PLANTS?

One of the most common problems experienced by new fish keepers is fish eating the aquarium plants. Although some fish are heavily herbivorous, the majority will not cause any major harm to plants if the conditions for plant growth are good and the plants in the aquarium are healthy and growing strongly. It is much more likely that the problem lies elsewhere and it simply appears that the fish are eating the plants.

▼ *The tinfoil barb* (Barbodes schwanenfeldii) *can grow quite large and disrupt aquarium plants.*

Keeping plants healthy

ROUTINE TANK MAINTENANCE

DAILY

- Check for any missing livestock, and examine the health of all the fish. Look for red marks on the body and gills, excess mucus, gasping, or unusual behavior.
- Check the water temperature.
- Make sure that the filter(s) and lights are working efficiently.

TWICE WEEKLY

- Gently disturb any fine-leaved plants, such as *Cabomba* and dense foreground species, such as hairgrass, to remove any trapped detritus, which can hinder photosynthesis.

WEEKLY

- Test the water for nitrites (NO_2), nitrates (NO_3), pH, and hardness.
- Remove dead leaves and other plant matter.
- Siphon out or remove any mulm from the top layer of substrate and replace the water removed during this process with new, dechlorinated water. This will also constitute a small water change, replacing minerals and helping to lower levels of nitrates and phosphates.
- Replenish liquid fertilizers after water changes according to the maker's instructions.
- Using an algae magnet, pad, or scraper, clean the inside front and side glass, even if little algae is present. This prevents a buildup of algae that can be hard to remove.
- If you have a condensation cover, wipe it clean to avoid a reduction in light penetration.

▶ *Rinse the sponge from an internal filter in a bowl of aquarium water.*

◀ *Use a siphon gravel cleaner to pick up detritus from the substrate.*

EVERY TWO WEEKS

- Thoroughly clean half the sponge in the internal filter, using water from the aquarium. Then discard it.

MONTHLY

- Switch off external filters and clean the media in water from the aquarium. Then discard the water.
- Replace any filter floss in an external filter.

EVERY THREE MONTHS

- Check the substrate for compaction and gently loosen it with your fingers.
- Remove and clean any impellers and impeller housings in pumps and filters.

EVERY 6–12 MONTHS

- If fluorescent tubes are the main source of lighting, replace them even if they are still working. After 10–12 months they will have lost much of their intensity.
- Replace filter sponges. Over time, the bacterial capacity of sponges diminishes and they need to be replaced. If sponges are the main biological medium, then replace half at a time, leaving a month in between. This will reduce the loss of bacteria.

WHEN NEEDED

- Replenish liquid or tablet fertilizers according to the maker's instructions.
- Check and replenish any CO_2 supply systems that may be in use in the aquarium.
- Trim any tall stem plants, so that they do not grow across the surface and block out light to other plants. Replant the cuttings if you wish to fill out your display.
- If tall-stemmed plants are looking thin near the base, remove them, cut off the upper halves, and replant.

▲ Trim plants back if they grow too near the surface. Remove large portions if needed.

- If the leaves of plants such as large *Echinodorus* spp. have grown too big, remove the outermost leaves and trim the roots slightly. The plant will respond by producing fresh, smaller leaves.
- Old plant leaves may become tattered or covered in algae. Remove them to prevent the spread of algae and to allow new leaves to grow.
- Over time, some plants will become old and begin to look less healthy. They stop growing and become tattered. If this happens, remove and replace them. Be sure to take out the entire rootstock, as any pieces left over may rot and pollute the substrate across the whole aquarium.

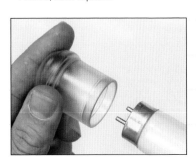

◀ To replace a tube, simply pull off the waterproof end caps.

▶ Fit a new one in the same way by aligning the pins.

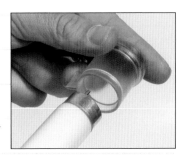

KEEPING PLANTS HEALTHY

Choosing suitable fish

Some aquarium fish can be damaging to plants, although nearly all fish appreciate a well-planted aquarium. Healthy plants provide hiding places, food, and territories, and they also help to make an aquarium a much better environment, in terms of water quality and aesthetics, for the fish. Many fish are also beneficial to plants, removing debris and cleaning the leaves of algae. A good selection of plants and fish will benefit each other and create a lively and interesting aquarium display for you to enjoy.

USEFUL ALGAE-EATING FISH FOR THE PLANTED AQUARIUM

Crossocheilus siamensis (Siamese flying fox)

Epalzeorhynchus bicolor (red-tailed black shark)

Epalzeorhynchus frenatus (ruby shark)

Farlowella acus (twig catfish)

Gastromyzon borneensis (hillstream loach)

Gyrinocheilus aymonieri (sucking loach)

Otocinclus affinis (dwarf otocinclus)

Peckoltia pulcher (dwarf plec)

Poecilia reticulata (guppy)

Poecilia sphenops (molly)

Poecilia velifera (sailfin molly)

Rineloricaria hasemania (whiptail catfish)

* *Plants provide useful hiding places and breeding sites for aquarium fish.*

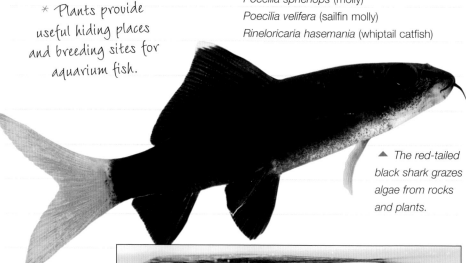

▲ *The red-tailed black shark grazes algae from rocks and plants.*

▶ *The marbled hatchetfish spends most of its time at the surface.*

USEFUL SCAVENGERS FOR THE PLANTED AQUARIUM

Acanthopsis choirorhynchus (horse-face loach)

Botia lohachata (Pakistani loach)

Botia macracantha (clown loach)

Botia striata (banded loach)

Corydoras spp. (corydoras catfish)

Pangio kuhlii (kuhli loach)

SURFACE SWIMMERS FOR THE PLANTED AQUARIUM

Betta splendens (Siamese fighting fish)

Carnegiella strigata (marbled hatchetfish)

Colisa lalia (dwarf gourami)

Colisa sota (honey gourami)

Kryptopterus bicirrhis (glass catfish)

Macropodus opercularis (paradisefish)

Poecilia reticulata (guppy)

Poecilia sphenops (molly)

Poecilia velifera (sailfin molly)

Thoracocharax stellatus (silver hatchetfish)

Trichopsis vittatus (croaking gourami)

Xiphophorus maculatus (platy)

▲ Corydoras *catfish are useful shoaling fish that will gently disturb the substrate.*

COMMON HERBIVOROUS FISH TO AVOID

Abramites (headstanders)

Distichodus

Leporinus

Metynnis (silver dollars)

Scatophagus (scats)

COMMON LARGE DESTRUCTIVE FISH TO AVOID

Barbodes schwanenfeldii (tinfoil barb)

Larger barbs

Central American cichlids

Rift Lake cichlids

Pterygoplichthys / Glyptoperichthys

Serrasalmus (piranhas, below)

Large *Synodontis*

Choosing suitable fish

When you are choosing fish for your planted aquarium, try to include some that will live in each of the three major zones: the surface waters, the midwater swimming area, and the bottom zone.

◀ *Zebra danios are constantly on the move and enjoy a strong water current in the aquarium.*

SMALL SHOALING FISH FOR A PLANTED AQUARIUM

Hemigrammus bleheri (rummy-nose tetra)

Hemigrammus erythrozonus (glowlight tetra)

Megalamphodus megalopterus (black phantom tetra)

Megalamphodus sweglesi (red phantom tetra)

Nematobrycon palmeri (emperor tetra)

Paracheirodon axelrodi (cardinal tetra)

Puntius titteya (cherry barb)

Rasbora heteromorpha (harlequin rasbora)

SMALL SHOALING FISH THAT PREFER A CURRENT

Brachydanio sp. (danios)

Hasemania nana (silver-tip tetra)

Tanichthys albonubes (White Cloud Mountain minnow)

OTHER SMALL FISH OF INTEREST

Apistogramma agassizi (Agassiz's dwarf cichlid)

Apistogramma borellii (yellow dwarf cichlid)

Apistogramma cacatuoides (cockatoo dwarf cichlid)

Apteronotus albifrons (white-tip black ghost knifefish)

Papiliochromis ramirezi (ram)

Pelvicachromis pulcher (kribensis)

Most tetras prefer slightly soft and acidic water, which also suits many plants.

▶ *Cardinal tetras add bright flashes of iridescent color to any planted aquarium.*

▼ Cockatoo dwarf cichlids (male top, female bottom) will grow to 2 in (5 cm).

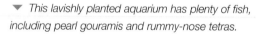

LARGER FISH SUITABLE FOR A PLANTED AQUARIUM

Ctenopoma maculata
  (marbled ctenopoma)
Mesonauta festivus (festive cichlid)
Pterophyllum scalare (angelfish)
Symphysodon discus (discus)
Trichogaster leeri (pearl gourami)
Trichogaster microlepis
  (moonlight gourami)
Trichogaster trichopterus
  (three-spot gourami)

▼ This lavishly planted aquarium has plenty of fish, including pearl gouramis and rummy-nose tetras.

Creating a display

The difference between a well-planted aquarium and a stunning display aquarium lies in good aquascaping. Aquascaping is not just a matter of placing plants and decor in the right combinations or in the right places; it means being creative, imaginative—even inspired. Aquarists are faced with a wide range of rocks, wood, and other decor, but not all materials are suitable for a planted aquarium. When making a choice, it is often best to keep things simple and stick to, say, one or two types of rock rather than crowd the aquarium with all manner of objects. All the decor should, of course, be bought and not collected from the wild. Clean it well before using it in the aquarium.

◀ *Cobbles create gaps between smaller plants and make open spaces more interesting.*

* Inert rocks are safe to use. Avoid chalk, limestone, marble, and tufa rock.

SAFE AND UNSAFE ROCKS

Stack granite pieces or use individually.

Quartz has an interesting color.

THE FIZZ TEST

To test if a rock is likely to alter water quality, pour on some acidic substance such as vinegar. If the rock contains any calcareous substance, it will begin to fizz gently.

Calcareous rocks are often brittle or porous. Do not use them in a planted aquarium.

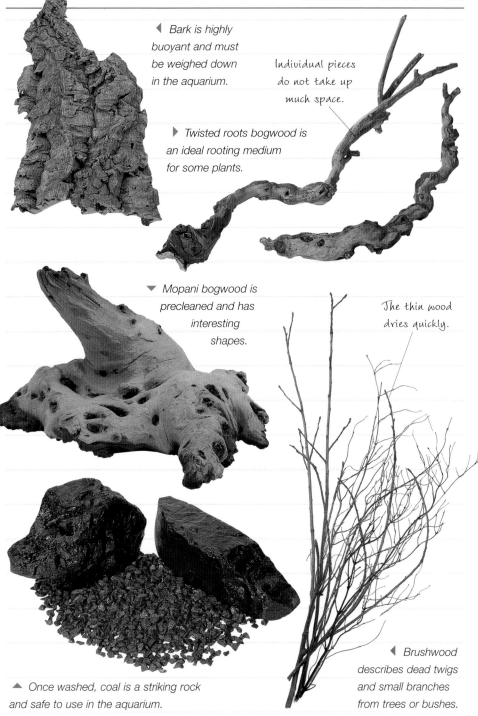

◀ Bark is highly buoyant and must be weighed down in the aquarium.

Individual pieces do not take up much space.

▶ Twisted roots bogwood is an ideal rooting medium for some plants.

▼ Mopani bogwood is precleaned and has interesting shapes.

The thin wood dries quickly.

▲ Once washed, coal is a striking rock and safe to use in the aquarium.

◀ Brushwood describes dead twigs and small branches from trees or bushes.

Creating a display

Providing you have access to a good range of materials, it is possible to design and create a good display on impulse, but results are often far better if you do some preplanning. Sketching out an overhead view of the aquarium allows you to plan the decor, assess the number of plants you will need and how they blend in with the filtration and other equipment. Divide the space into background, midground, and foreground areas, and choose plants for each area. You might like to consider setting up a themed tank, such as those shown on pages 56–63.

◀ For underwater protection, paint bamboo cane and other woods inside and out with clear polyurethane varnish.

▼ Fake bark, bogwood, wood, and rock are safe to use in planted tanks.

▲ Using different sizes and lengths of bamboo adds variety.

* Artificial equivalents look very realistic once they are covered in a slight algal growth.

◀ Freshwater mussels look at home amongst the plants in a European lake display. Although generally static, they do move around and are interesting creatures to observe. Offer these filter feeders daphnia and plankton-based foods sold for marine aquariums.

▶ By using bogwood and other large pieces of decor, and filling in behind them with a suitable substrate material, you can create raised planting beds.

Lime-free and pea gravel

SKETCHING A PLAN

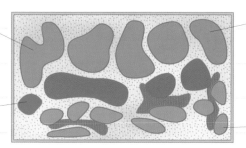

Background
Place tall and/or bushy plants in large groups toward the back.

Back/midground
Stem plants or plants on bogwood make good middle to background plants.

Specimen/Unusual
Single, large species plants may require their own space as display plants.

Foreground
Place smaller plants amongst small rocks and pebbles.

Plants for the aquarium

BACKGROUND
Alternanthera reineckii
Ammannia gracilis
Anubias barteri var. barteri
Anubias congensis
Aponogeton ulvaceus
Bacopa caroliniana
Barclaya longifolia
Blyxa echinosperma
Bolbitis heudelotii
Cabomba sp.
Ceratophyllum demersum
Ceratopteris cornuta
Crinum natans
Crinum thaianum
Cryptocoryne balansae
Cryptocoryne undulata
Cryptocoryne wendtii
Echinodorus amazonicus
Echinodorus bleheri
Echinodorus cordifolius
Echinodorus grandiflorus
Echinodorus macrophyllus
Echinodorus major
Echinodorus osiris
Echinodorus parviflorus
Echinodorus uruguayensis
Egeria densa
Elodea canadensis
Eusteralis stellata
Gymnocoronis spilanthoides
Heteranthera zosterifolia
Hygrophila corymbosa
Hygrophila difformis
Hygrophila guianensis
Hygrophila polysperma
Limnophila aquatica
Limnophila sessiliflora
Ludwigia glandulosa

Ludwigia repens
Ludwigia palustris
Microsorium pteropus
Myriophyllum sp.
Najas indica
Nesaea crassicaulis
Nuphar japonica
Nymphaea lotus
Potamogeton crispus
Rotala macrandra
Rotala rotundifolia
Sagittaria subulata
Shinnersia rivularis
Spathiphyllum wallisii
Vallisneria americana
Vallisneria asiatica var.
    biwaensis
Vallisneria gigantea
Vallisneria spiralis

MIDGROUND
Alternanthera reineckii
Ammannia gracilis
Anubias angustifolia "Afzelii"
Anubias barteri var. barteri
Anubias gracilis
Anubias lanceolata

Aponogeton boivinianus
Aponogeton crispus
Aponogeton
    madagascariensis
Aponogeton ulvaceus
Bacopa caroliniana
Bacopa monnieri
Barclaya longifolia
Blyxa echinosperma
Blyxa japonica
Bolbitis heudelotii
Cardamine lyrata
Ceratophyllum demersum
Cryptocoryne affinis
Cryptocoryne balansae
Cryptocoryne beckettii
Cryptocoryne lutea
Cryptocoryne pontederiifolia
Cryptocoryne undulata
Cryptocoryne walkeri
Cryptocoryne wendtii
Didiplis diandra
Echinodorus amazonicus
Echinodorus cordifolius
Echinodorus horemanii
Echinodorus osiris

Nesaea
crassicaulis

Hydrocotyle
leucocephala

Echinodorus parviflorus
Echinodorus uruguayensis
Egeria densa
Eichhornia azurea
Eleocharis acicularis
Eleocharis parvula
Eleocharis vivipara
Eusteralis stellata
Fontinalis antipyretica
Gymnocoronis spilanthoides
Hemianthus
    micranthemoides
Heteranthera zosterifolia
Hydrocotyle leucocephala
Hydrocotyle sibthorpioides
Hydrocotyle verticillata
Hygrophila corymbosa
Hygrophila guianensis
Lagarosiphon major
Limnophila sessiliflora
Lobelia cardinalis
Ludwigia repens
Ludwigia palustris
Lysimachia nummularia
Microsorium pteropus
Myriophyllum sp.
Najas indica
Nuphar japonica
Nymphaea lotus
Nymphaea stellata
Nymphoides aquatica
Potamogeton crispus

Rotala macrandra
Rotala rotundifolia
Sagittaria platyphylla
Sagittaria subulata
Saururus cernuus
Shinnersia rivularis
Spathiphyllum wallisii
Vallisneria americana
Vallisneria tortifolia

FOREGROUND
Anubias angustifolia "Afzelii"
Anubias barteri var. nana
Anubias gracilis
Anubias lanceolata
Aponogeton crispus
Aponogeton
    madagascariensis
Aponogeton undulatus
Bacopa monnieri
Bacopa rotundifolia
Blyxa japonica
Cardamine lyrata
Cryptocoryne affinis
Cryptocoryne balansae
Cryptocoryne beckettii
Cryptocoryne lutea
Cryptocoryne parva
Cryptocoryne pontederiifolia
Cryptocoryne undulata
Cryptocoryne walkeri
Cryptocoryne willisii

Didiplis diandra
Echinodorus bolivianus
Echinodorus tenellus
Eleocharis acicularis
Eusteralis stellata
Fontinalis antipyretica
Glossostigma elatinoides
Hemianthus callitrichoides
Heteranthera zosterifolia
Hydrocotyle leucocephala
Hydrocotyle sibthorpioides
Hydrocotyle verticillata
Lagarosiphon major
Lilaeopsis novae-zelandiae
Lobelia cardinalis
Lysimachia nummularia
Marsilea hirsuta
Micranthemum umbrosum
Nymphoides aquatica
Sagittaria platyphylla
Sagittaria pusilla
Samolus valerandi
Saururus cernuus
Vallisneria tortifolia
Vesicularia dubyana

FLOATING
Azolla sp.
Ceratophyllum demersum
Ceratopteris cornuta
Eichhornia crassipes
Hydrocotyle leucocephala
Limnobium laevigatum
Ludwigia helminthorrhiza
Micranthemum umbrosum
Najas indica
Nymphoides aquatica
Pistia stratiotes
Riccia fluitans
Salvinia sp.
Trapa natans

Themed tanks

A PALUDARIUM

In a paludarium, the design focuses on a combination of above and below water environments. A typical paludarium will be no more than a third to half full, so you will need a relatively tall aquarium to ensure that there is enough space above and below the water. The plants can be a mixture of aquatic, terrestrial, and marsh species, but all should do well in moist conditions. Mosses and ferns are well suited to paludariums. This example features only aquatic and marsh plants. The most vital part of the construction is ensuring that the rockwork is secure, so anchor it all firmly with silicone sealant before filling the tank. Good ventilation is also important to prevent the air from overheating and damaging plant leaves. Use an air pump to create small currents of moving air above the water.

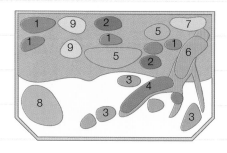

PLANT LIST

1. *Acorus gramineus* var. *pusillus* (Dwarf Japanese rush)
2. *Anubias lanceolata* (Narrow-leaved anubias)
3. *Cryptocoryne* spp.
4. *Anubias barteri* var. *nana*
5. *Lysimachia nummularia* (Creeping Jenny)
6. *Microsorium pteropus* (Java fern)
7. *Ophiopogon japonicus* "Variegatus" (Variegated fountain plant)
8. *Spathiphyllum wallisii* (Peace lily)
9. *Syngonium podophyllum* (Stardust ivy)

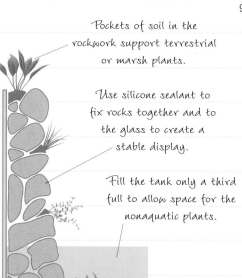

Pockets of soil in the rockwork support terrestrial or marsh plants.

Use silicone sealant to fix rocks together and to the glass to create a stable display.

Fill the tank only a third full to allow space for the nonaquatic plants.

AN OPEN-TOPPED AQUARIUM

The water surface of an aquarium without a hood can be used as an extension of the display. Floating plants and leaves produced above the water add an extra element. If the aquarium is large enough, you can also include bogwood and houseplants. An open-topped aquarium must be illuminated with pendant-type lighting. If plants are to grow on or above the water surface, allow enough space (at least 18 in/45 cm) between the light and the water surface so that the leaves do not overheat. For the same reason, provide good ventilation. If the light source is very hot, it may be worth carefully positioning a small fan to create a cooling air current above the aquarium.

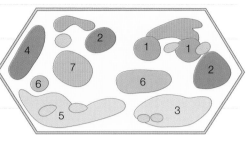

PLANT LIST

1. *Anubias congensis* (Congo anubias)
2. *Cabomba piauhyensis* (Red cabomba)
3. *Cryptocoryne parva*
4. *Echinodorus grandiflorus* (Large-flowered Amazon swordplant)
5. *Echinodorus tenellus* (Pygmy chain swordplant)
6. *Nuphar japonica* (Spatterdock)
7. *Nymphaea lotus* var. *rubra* (Red tiger lotus)

Echinodorus grandiflorus is ideal for large, open-top tanks.

FLOATING PLANTS

Pistia stratiotes (Water lettuce)
Salvinia auriculata (Salvinia)

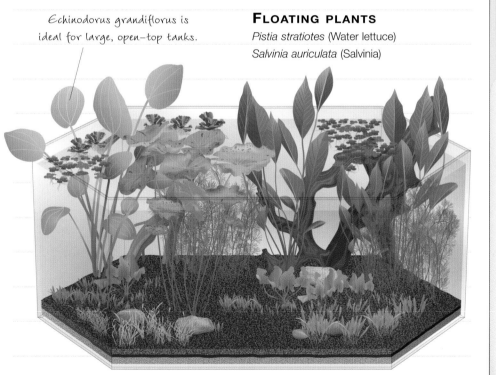

Themed tanks

A COLD WATER AQUARIUM

It is true to say that well-planted cold water aquariums are rarely seen, although there are plenty of plants available that prefer colder water. Many of these are sold alongside tropical plants and also do well in warmer water. Another place to look for suitable plants for an unheated aquarium is amongst submerged or marginal pond plants. If you do use these, be sure to remove the aquatic soil they are planted in, as it will muddy the aquarium water.

An unheated or cold water aquarium kept indoors rarely becomes very cold, often stabilizing at about 64–72° F (18–22° C), and should more accurately be described as a temperate aquarium. It may be worth investing in a Heaterstat for a cold water aquarium to prevent temperatures from fluctuating, which can adversely affect both fish and plants.

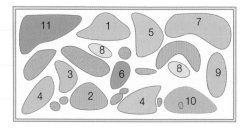

PLANT LIST

1. *Egeria densa* (Elodea)
2. *Eleocharis parvula* (Dwarf hairgrass)
3. *Gymnocoronis spilanthoides* (Spadeleaf plant)
4. *Hydrocotyle verticillata* (Whorled umbrella plant)
5. *Ludwigia palustris* (Broadleaf ludwigia)
6. *Lysimachia nummularia* (Creeping Jenny)
7. *Myriophyllum hippuroides* (Green milfoil)
8. *Nuphar japonica* (Spatterdock)
9. *Potamogeton crispus*
10. *Sagittaria platyphylla* (Giant sagittaria)
11. *Vallisneria spiralis* (Straight vallis)

Vallisneria spiralis

A HARD WATER AQUARIUM

Depending on where you live, your water may be hard and alkaline (high pH). Although it is possible to remove hardness and soften water with proprietary chemicals and filtration systems, it can be costly and time-consuming. Most plants do best in medium-soft water and although many will acclimate to harder water for short periods, in the long-term, hard water will damage them and adversely affect their growth. However, there are hard water areas in the wild where plants thrive, and the importance of soft water in planted aquariums is debatable as far as these species are concerned. A few plants survive notably better in harder water; a typical example is elodea or pondweed *(Egeria densa)*. Adding CO_2 in hard water conditions is an excellent idea, as it will slightly acidify the water and compensate for the drop in available nutrients.

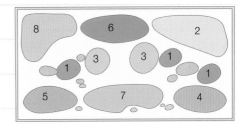

PLANT LIST

1. *Aponogeton elongatus* (Elongated swordplant)
2. *Cabomba caroliniana* (Green cabomba)
3. *Cardamine lyrata* (Chinese ivy)
4. *Cryptocoryne walkeri*
5. *Cryptocoryne wendtii*
6. *Hygrophila stricta* (Thai stricta)
7. *Sagittaria pusilla* (Dwarf sagittaria)
8. *Vallisneria asiatica* var. *biwaensis* (Twisted, or corkscrew, vallisneria)

Cabomba caroliniana is easy to keep in harder water.

Themed tanks

A LOW-LIGHT AQUARIUM

In some situations, providing suitably intense light may be costly or impractical. Luckily for the aquarist, there are plants that thrive in shady streams with little natural light, and these plants have adapted to grow in relatively dim conditions. Indeed, some of them will not do well if given too much light.

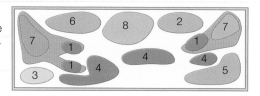

One limitation of low-light conditions is that suitable foreground plants are hard to obtain. Because foreground plants are low growing, they do not receive as much light as taller plants nearer the water surface. This means that most foreground plants require a more intense light source in the aquarium. The exceptions are many *Cryptocoryne* species, which come from shallow streams, often shaded by terrestrial vegetation.

Slow-growing plants generally have a slow metabolism, so they have less need of light energy. The plants in this display can be kept in a tank with one or two fluorescent tubes.

PLANT LIST

1. *Anubias barteri* var. *nana* (Dwarf anubias)
2. *Ceratophyllum demersum* (Hornwort)
3. *Cryptocoryne affinis*
4. *Cryptocoryne lutea*
5. *Cryptocoryne walkeri*
6. *Egeria densa* (Elodea)
7. *Microsorium pteropus* (Java fern)
8. *Hygrophila corymbosa*

FLOATING PLANT

Salvinia auriculata (Salvinia)

Ceratophyllum demersum

Salvinia auriculata casts natural shade.

AN INDONESIAN STREAM

In the rain forests of Indonesia there are many small tropical streams, often slow moving and swamplike, with overhanging vegetation creating light and dark patches. A number of aquatic plants flourish in the iron-rich reddish substrate, which is interspersed with small pebbles and stones. Many of the species for this biotope are slow growing and do not require strong light, making this biotope an ideal one for beginners to attempt. However, not all the plants from this region will do well without strong lighting. Many are found in areas with little overhanging vegetation, where intense sunlight penetrates the shallow waters.

The red substrate often found in these types of streams is the result of iron, and can be recreated using a reddish brown gravel. Water quality should be neutral to soft (pH 6.8–7.2), with a temperature of 77–80° F (25–27° C). Provide additional CO_2.

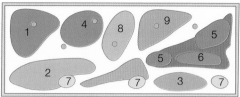

PLANT LIST

1. *Blyxa echinosperma* (Giant Japanese rush)
2. *Cryptocoryne affinis*
3. *Cryptocoryne moehlmannii* (Moehlmann's cryptocoryne)
4. *Hygrophila corymbosa* "Crispa"
5. *Microsorium pteropus* (Java fern)
6. *Vesicularia dubyana (Java moss)*
7. *Cryptocoryne balansae*
8. *Rotala wallichii* (Whorly rotala)
9. *Rotala rotundifolia*

Bamboo canes and bogwood create good focal points in this display.

Blyxa echinosperma

Themed tanks

A MOUNTAIN STREAM

The mountain streams found at the source of many rivers are inhospitable places for aquatic plants. Fast-moving water constantly batters the leaves and removes useful nutrients, while high oxygen levels make life hard for many plants. However, a few species are highly adaptable and, although sparse, are readily found in such environments. To imitate this biotope, use large, rounded gravel for the top layer of the aquarium substrate, plus a number of cobbles or rocks. Installing overpowered filtration or additional pumps will recreate the fast-flowing water.

Carbon dioxide systems would be ineffective in this type of aquarium, as the increased air/water exchange would remove much of the CO_2 as soon as it was introduced. Instead, use liquid fertilizers to

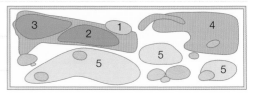

PLANT LIST

1. *Bolbitis heudelotii* (African fern)
2. *Fontinalis antipyretica* (Willow moss)
3. *Microsorium pteropus* (Java fern)
4. *Vallisneria gigantea* (Giant vallisneria)
5. *Sagittaria pusilla* (Dwarf sagittaria)

replace any substrate fertilization. Water quality is relatively unimportant to both fish and plants in this biotope. Recreating this habitat in a tank results in a poor environment for most aquatic plants, but providing you choose the correct group of plants, you can be successful and achieve a dramatic effect.

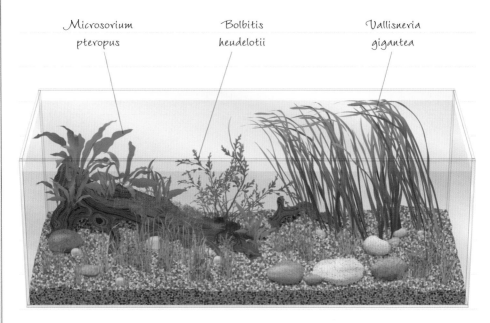

Microsorium pteropus

Bolbitis heudelotii

Vallisneria gigantea

AN AFRICAN POOL

Two main styles of aquarium can be recreated here. The fast, open waters of the Zaire River, for example, are home to few plants, since the high oxygen levels and rapid waters make conditions unsuitable for many species. This type of display would resemble a mountain stream biotope. By contrast, the lowland swamps, pools and slow-moving streams found in many places, often by the sides of faster moving waters, are filled with aquatic plants. Along the muddy banks, species of *Azolla, Eleocharis acicularis*, and *Ceratopteris* grow in dense clumps in the nutrient-rich water and substrate. Temperatures in these areas can approach 86° F (30° C), although these temperatures need not be recreated in the aquarium. For best results, provide soft water with a pH between 6 and 6.8 (acidic to slightly acidic).

This aquarium represents the deeper area of a pool. The lack of water movement and large fish make it a suitable environment for delicate-leaved species, such as *Ammannia*

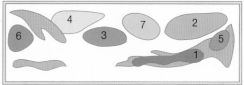

PLANT LIST

1. *Anubias barteri* var. *nana*
2. *Ammannia gracilis*
   (Delicate ammannia)
3. *Bacopa monnieri* (Dwarf bacopa)
4. *Barclaya longifolia* (Orchid lily)
5. *Bolbitis heudelotii* (African fern)
6. *Crinum natans* (African onion plant)
7. *Lagarosiphon major*
   (African waterweed)

and *Barclaya* spp. The broken branches and wood often found in these pools can be represented by bogwood, which also releases tannic acids, helping to keep the pH level low. Many of the plants used here may need good lighting and a supply of liquid fertilizer.

THEMED TANKS

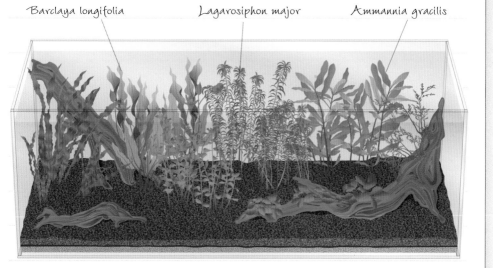

Barclaya longifolia   *Lagarosiphon major*   *Ammannia gracilis*

Putting it all together

There are many styles of aquarium design, from barren rockscapes to heavily and diversely planted "Dutch-style" aquariums. You could be inspired by such designs or simply use your own, but in either case it is important to stick to a single style within one aquarium. When using rocks, select one or two types and use them in various sizes, rather than mix several different types of rocks and individual pieces. The same applies to wood; it is generally better to use one type than many. Plant species, on the other hand, can be used either singly, in small groups, or in large groups. A stunning aquarium can be created using 1 species, 2 species, or 30 species! Individual plant species all have a place. Taller stem plants and large-leaved species work well as background plants, while smaller plants can be used in the midground, with low-growing species in the foreground. However, there are no set rules for what constitutes a foreground or background plant, and it is often better to mix up the areas a little. Generally speaking, a larger plant should be placed behind a small one for obvious reasons, but plants can be grouped and placed in a number of ways to create an interesting design.

▲ In this aquarium, large Amazon swordplants provide a bold accent in the background. In the midground area, cryptocorynes soften the edges of the rocks and lead the eye to the low plants in the foreground.

* Although it is tempting to use many different species, it is often easier and more effective to use a limited number of species in larger groupings.

POPULAR AQUARIUM PLANTS

Aquarists are lucky in that there are literally hundreds of plant species suitable for aquarium conditions. Not all these plants are found in nature; many are cultivated varieties developed by plant growers, wholesalers, and, in some cases, individual aquarists. As a result of crossbreeding and selective propagation, we can now choose from a wide range of plants with varied and interesting leaf shapes, colors, growth patterns, and care requirements. Many plants also have subspecies, which are usually slightly different in height or leaf shape.

Most aquatic outlets stock a good selection of aquarium plants, which should vary slightly from week to week. But what happens if you are looking for a certain species or type of plant? If you are having difficulty obtaining a particular plant, you may find that one of the many mail-order suppliers will stock it or something similar. Alternatively, your local retailers may be able to locate it from one of their suppliers.

Although welcome, this wide selection of aquarium plants can be quite daunting. Where do you start? In this section of the book, we present a wide range of plants grouped according to how they are best used in an aquarium: background, midground, foreground, and floating. However, there are many other ways of grouping plants and drawing up a short list of suitable species by a process of elimination. For example, plants can be selected for suitability by their height, spread, lighting, and nutrient and temperature requirements. Or you can simply choose plants based on their colors, size, and leaf shapes. Plants in the aquarium should both contrast and complement each other, although choosing plants in this way is purely a matter of taste. However, a planted aquarium is not a static display, and plants can be moved around, swapped about, trimmed, propagated, or removed as required. Choosing the right plants needs time and thought, although mistakes are easily remedied. Using this guide, you will find it easy to select a range of plants to create your own "living picture."

Background plants

The plants along the back of the aquarium should all be tall-growing species, and groups often look better than individual plants. On the other hand, bushy-stemmed plants, such as *Cabomba*, *Limnophila*, or *Myriophyllum* species, make good background plants when grouped together, and they combine well with adjacent tall but small-leaved stem plants such as *Bacopa*.

▼ Cabomba caroliniana *thrives even in hard water conditions and moderate light.*

▲ *The slow-growing* Anubias barteri *var.* caladiifolia *"1705" is hardy and adaptable.*

◀ *In strong light and an iron-rich substrate,* Alternanthera reineckii *is easy to care for.*

▲ *Wavy-edged leaves are typical of* Aponogeton *species. This is* A. ulvaceus.

FOOD IN RESERVE

In many aquatic plants, the base of the stem is adapted into a rhizome, bulb, or tuber. These are found in plants such as *Aponogeton*, *Anubias*, *Crinum* and *Echinodorus* species. The plants can draw on the food reserves in these storage organs to survive harsh periods.

▲ *The leaves of* Ceratopteris cornuta *vary in shape depending on aquarium conditions.*

▲ *The tough leaves of* Crinum thaianum *will survive the attentions of boisterous or herbivorous fish. Once at the surface, they float horizontally.*

◀ *In clean water, good light, and fine substrate,* Bacopa caroliniana *grows to 16 in (40 cm).*

BACKGROUND PLANTS

Background plants

In the larger aquarium, big-leaved plants, such as many of the larger *Echinodorus* species, can be used either singly or in well-spaced groups. If given enough space and an open top, they will quickly produce leaves (and flowers) above the surface. *Echinodorus* species propagate by producing daughter plants on runners, which can be separated and planted individually.

▶ *The red-dappled leaves and bold shape of Echinodorus "Red Flame" provide a bold focal point.*

* There are more than 45 species of Echinodorus in the wild and many are available for aquariums.

▼ Echinodorus palaefolius *var.* latifolius *makes an excellent specimen plant, growing up to 16 in (40 cm).*

▼ Echinodorus barthii *slowly attains a height of 8–10 in (20–25 cm).*

In good light, the leaves are golden red.

Attractive veined leaves.

Flowers on runners develop into daughter plants that can be removed and replanted.

▲ Echinodorus "Oriental" is a cultivated hybrid that must have bright light and plenty of nutrients.

◀ The distinctive leaves of Echinodorus "Rubin" are a mixture of red and green areas.

Visible veins add to the interest of this cultivated variety.

In good conditions, the plant produces adventitious plantlets on runners.

▶ Once established, Echinodorus bleheri can take up a lot of space, so use it with care. Provide iron in the substrate and through liquid fertilizers.

BACKGROUND PLANTS

Background plants

Growth rates vary among plant species, but in ideal conditions most background plants are fast-growing and need regular pruning and/or thinning to keep them tidy. Cuttings can be replanted in the substrate and should quickly produce roots. Good lighting, CO_2, and iron fertilization are important for good growth.

▼ Heteranthera zosterifolia *is a tall, bushy plant that is ideal for the back of a display. It grows to 20 in (50 cm).*

▲ *Fast-growing* Egeria densa *is highly adaptable and very easy to keep.*

▼ *The fleshy leaves of* Gymnocoronis spilanthoides *can grow 5.5 in (14 cm) long, so allow space between stems when planting.*

BACKGROUND PLANTS

◀ Hygrophila difformis *prospers in bright light. Plant it in well-spaced groups.*

▼ *"Siamensis" is a narrow-leaved form of* Hygrophila corymbosa.

▼ Hygrophila polysperma *"Rosenervig" is one of several varieties available for aquariums.*

Hygrophila species vary in leaf form.

▼ *For best results, give* Hygrophila guianensis *space, light, and nutrients.*

Background plants

When choosing plants for the aquarium, particularly large ones for the background, it is important to make sure that each will thrive in the same water quality. Find out as much as you can about each plant, including where and how it grows in the wild, before creating mixed displays.

◀ Limnophila aquatica, *a native of India and Sri Lanka, appreciates fairly soft water and a source of iron.*

▶ Microsorium pteropus *(Java fern) is versatile, easy to keep, and it requires little light.*

▼ *The leaves of* Ludwigia repens *are an attractive reddish color on the underside.*

The roots attach to rocks and wood.

* Black spots on the underside of leaves may not indicate damage. They are often spores from which new plants will grow.

▶ ▼ *If the small leaves of the finely branched* Microsorium pteropus *"Windelov" are nibbled by fish, the effect is less noticeable than on a large-leaved plant.*

▼ *The intense olive green/pink leaves of* Ludwigia glandulosa *stand out well in a brightly lit planted aquarium.*

NATURAL DEFENSE

The leaves of Java fern contain a chemical that deters most herbivorous fish from eating it. However, large destructive fish, such as oscars or tinfoil barbs, may still destroy leaves without eating them!

BACKGROUND PLANTS

Background plants

To get the best from many background plants, it is vital to provide strong lighting in the aquarium. In these conditions, background plants will develop into well-shaped plants with intense colors. Plants with brown or red foliage need the strongest light to maintain their vivid display. Space plants to allow light to reach the lower leaves.

▲ *Keep* Myriophyllum aquaticum *in water that is clear of visible debris, otherwise the fine leaves become clogged.*

▼ *The brown red color of* Myriophyllum tuberculatum *is unusual among common aquarium plants.*

Provide strong light to maintain the leaf color.

The leaves resemble seaweed.

◀ Potamogeton crispus, *a cold-water plant, needs strong lighting and a good, iron-rich substrate.*

▲ Nymphaea lotus *is ideal as a display species in large aquariums and makes a fine centerpiece in small tanks. Provide bright light.*

▶ Nesaea crassicaulis *requires slightly soft water and strong lighting.*

The plant can grow to 16–20 in (40–50 cm).

Background plants

Be adventurous when choosing plants that form the main elements of your aquarium display. Vary the leaf shape and color, and even include some nonaquatic plants, such as the peace lily *(Spathiphyllum wallisii)*. For themed aquariums, select species that reflect a particular environment, such as a flowing river, quiet forest pool, or brackish estuary.

▶ *The stunning deep red leaf color of* Rotala macrandra *is dependent on strong lighting and iron-rich fertilizer. Handle the delicate stems with care.*

▼ Shinnersia rivularis *"Weiss Grün," can reach the surface and continue to grow underwater.*

Attractive oak-leaf shaped foliage

USING NONAQUATIC PLANTS

Several decorative terrestrial plants are often for sale alongside true aquarium species. Most of these nonaquatic plants naturally grow in areas that are occasionally flooded or permanently marshy and will survive for extended periods underwater. Many have unusual leaf forms or colors not found in true aquatic plants and thus extend the choices available to aquarists.

▶ ▲ *Although not a true aquatic plant,*
Spathiphyllum wallisii *will survive submerged
and remain healthy for many months,
sometimes years. Beautiful white flowers
readily form on healthy specimens.*

▼ *The small-leaved* Rotala rotundifolia
*has an attractive, delicate appearance.
It is ideal for planting in groups.*

Background plants

In areas of water flow, such as near the filter outlet, the best background plants are those with long, narrow leaves. They are suited to the disturbance, and they create an element of movement in the aquarium. *Vallisneria* species, with their strap-shaped and often twisted leaves, are ideal.

◀ *A spiral flower stem winds its way upward amid the elegant, straplike leaves of* Vallisneria natans.

▶ *The fleshy leaves of* Vallisneria gigantea *may reach up to 39in (1m) in length and will trail across the water surface.*

✳ The tiny white flowers of Vallisneria are often produced in the aquarium and may be formed on a straight or twisted stem.

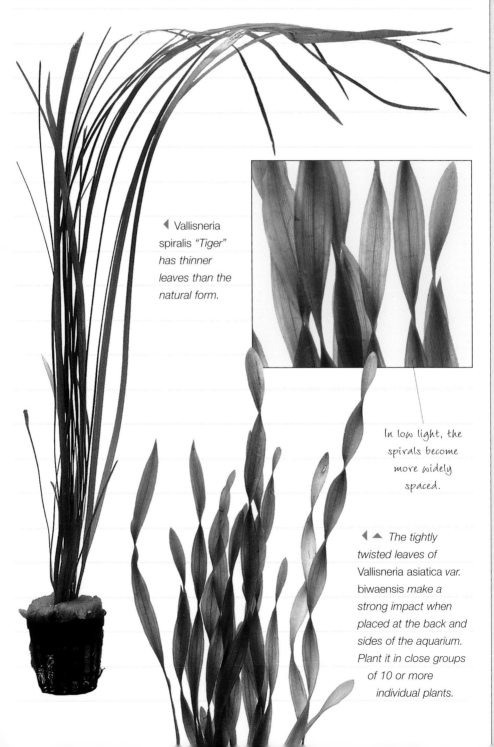

◀ Vallisneria spiralis *"Tiger"* has thinner leaves than the natural form.

In low light, the spirals become more widely spaced.

◀ ▲ *The tightly twisted leaves of* Vallisneria asiatica var. biwaensis *make a strong impact when placed at the back and sides of the aquarium. Plant it in close groups of 10 or more individual plants.*

BACKGROUND PLANTS

Midground plants

The midground is an undefined area—simply a mixing of the foreground and background. Plants that can be trimmed to variable heights are ideal here. Specimen plants can also look at home in the midground, providing they have sufficient space. In average-sized tanks, just a few specimen plants will make an impact.

▶ *The attractive, bright green, crinkled leaf and large size of* Aponogeton boivinianus *make it an ideal specimen plant for the midground of a larger aquarium.*

▼ Anubias angustifolia *"Afzelii" is an attractive thick-leaved plant that is tough enough to withstand the attentions of boisterous or herbivorous fish.*

Aponogeton are grown from bulbs that store large amounts of nutrients.

* *Anubias come from rivers and streams in Africa, where they are found along the edges and in marsh conditions.*

▶ Bolbitis heudelotii, *a slow-growing fern, is often sold attached to bogwood. Place it in areas of water movement.*

◀ Cardamine lyrata *looks best in small groups of three or four stems in between smaller, low-growing foreground plants.*

▲ *Not only is* Aponogeton crispus *adaptable and easy to grow but it also has attractive olive green/brown ruffled leaves and may even flower in the aquarium.*

MIDGROUND PLANTS

Midground plants

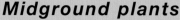

Cryptocoryne are among the most popular and widely available aquarium plants. Depending on their size, they are ideal for planting in the midground and foreground areas. In nature, Cryptocoryne come from a wide range of habitats, including shallow rivers, marshy areas, bogs, and swamps. All will adapt to fully submerged conditions.

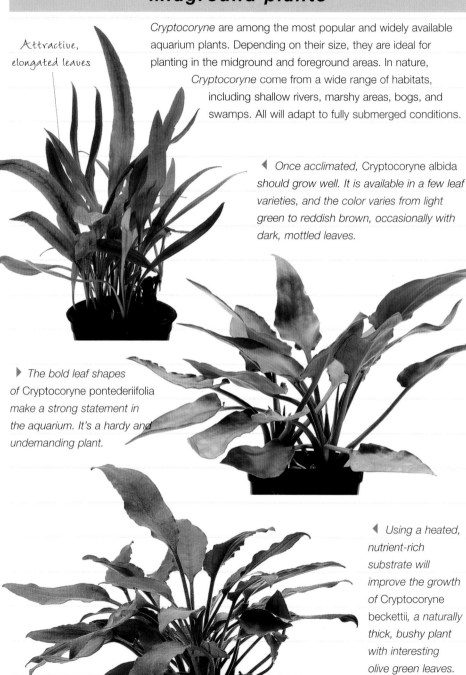

Attractive, elongated leaves

◀ *Once acclimated, Cryptocoryne albida should grow well. It is available in a few leaf varieties, and the color varies from light green to reddish brown, occasionally with dark, mottled leaves.*

▶ *The bold leaf shapes of Cryptocoryne pontederiifolia make a strong statement in the aquarium. It's a hardy and undemanding plant.*

◀ *Using a heated, nutrient-rich substrate will improve the growth of Cryptocoryne beckettii, a naturally thick, bushy plant with interesting olive green leaves.*

◀ Cryptocoryne undulata *produces long, dark-green, highly ruffled leaves that may grow to more than 14 in (35 cm).*

▼ *Widely available and easy to keep,* Cryptocoryne walkeri *var.* lutea *thrives in stable conditions.*

MIDGROUND PLANTS

▲ *The distinctive leaves of* Cryptocoryne balansae *are elongated and highly indented.*

▼ *Planting* Cryptocoryne wendtii *in spaced groups allows it to spread and create a dense clump.*

Midground plants

Creating a "street" grouping of one particular plant, with taller specimens in the background and others gradually becoming shorter toward the foreground, is a very effective and visually appealing method of blending areas together. Stem plants with many large or long leaves are excellent for this purpose.

✳ Echinodorus is one of the easiest plant groups to care for in the aquarium.

▶ Echinodorus quadricostatus var. xinguensis *adapts to different levels of light, and the length of the thin leaves vary according to light intensity. In good conditions, it grows and spreads quickly.*

▼ *Apart from good lighting and a supply of nutrients,* Hemianthus micranthemoides *has few requirements and adapts to most water conditions.*

GIVING PLANTS A CHANCE

Most aquarium plants are relatively easy to grow and soon become established. Some, however, need more time. To give them a chance, it is a good idea to introduce the slow-establishing plants before the more rampant species (which will rapidly use up available nutrients) and to give them additional help in the form of substrate fertilizer tablets.

▲ Eusteralis stellata *is challenging to grow, but it can make an impressive display.*

▼ *The shoots of* Hydrocotyle leucocephala *quickly reach the surface.*

Midground plants

Some plants available for use in the aquarium are pond plants, such as *Saururus* or forms of garden plants, such as *Lobelia*. This means that they can thrive in colder water and will be suitable for temperate aquarium displays.

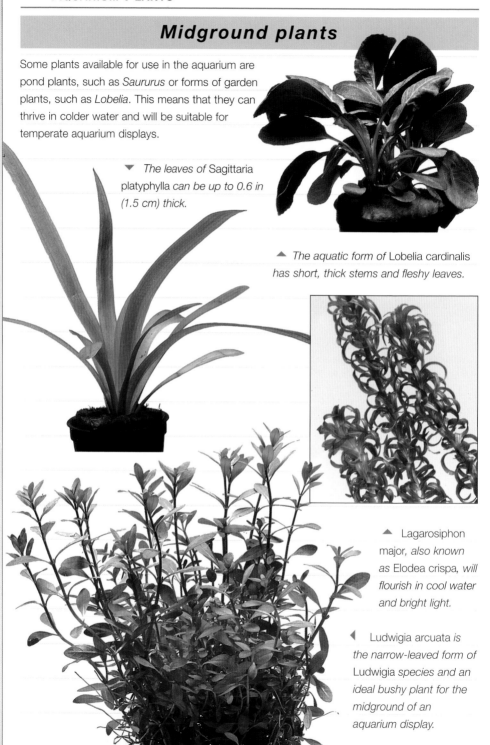

▼ *The leaves of* Sagittaria platyphylla *can be up to 0.6 in (1.5 cm) thick.*

▲ *The aquatic form of* Lobelia cardinalis *has short, thick stems and fleshy leaves.*

▲ Lagarosiphon major, *also known as* Elodea crispa, *will flourish in cool water and bright light.*

◀ Ludwigia arcuata *is the narrow-leaved form of* Ludwigia *species and an ideal bushy plant for the midground of an aquarium display.*

The oval to heart-shaped leaves of
Saururus cernuus will form above
each other in a spiral pattern.

▶ Given adequate
fertilization and bright
lighting, Saururus cernus
slowly grows to become a
fine specimen plant.

▲ Tolerant of a wide range of
conditions, Lysimachia nummularia
is ideal for the cold-water aquarium.

▶ Vallisneria tortifolia *spreads rapidly,
producing daughter plants from runners.*

MIDGROUND PLANTS

Foreground plants

The foreground of the aquarium provides an open swimming area and should occupy at least a third to half the available space. Depending on the size of the tank, one or two "carpet-forming" plant species can cover an open substrate area without intruding on the swimming space.

◀ *The compact* Anubias barteri var. nana *is an ideal foreground plant and will grow on a rock or piece of bogwood.*

▼ *Only 2 in (5 cm) high,* Cryptocoryne willisii *"Lucens" will spread out well.*

▲ *Grasslike* Eleocharis acicularis *needs clean water and bright light to thrive.*

▼ Echinodorus tenellus *sends out runners to create a lawnlike carpet.*

The aquatic leaves are finer than in the terrestrial form.

▲ *The tiny* Cryptocoryne parva *from Sri Lanka looks effective in groups along the foreground.*

* *Avoid placing foreground plants in shaded or covered areas.*

▼ Glossostigma elatinoides *can form a dense carpet only 0.6 in (1.5 cm) high.*

FOREGROUND PLANTS

Foreground plants

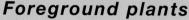

The foreground is a good site for individual specimen plants (such as *Anubias barteri* growing on a piece of bogwood) either in their own space or amongst carpet-forming species. Smaller pieces of bogwood or small stones and pebbles add further interest.

▼ Marsilea hirsuta *from Australia is an adaptable plant suited to a wide range of tank conditions.*

▲ *Bright lighting and good feeding will encourage* Hemianthus callitrichoides *to form a dense mat of deep green leaves. It can be pruned to maintain shape.*

Trim messy growth for better shape.

▶ *Small-leaved* Micranthemum umbrosum *is easy to grow.*

BREEDING SANCTUARY

Java moss *(Vesicularia dubyana)* from Asia forms a mass of shoots with tiny leaves that will spread in all directions. It is usually grown attached to rocks or bogwood. It is an ideal plant for a breeding tank, where the newly laid eggs will nestle out of harm's way.

▲ *Provide plenty of space and a stable environment for* Samolus valerandi.

Circular leaves 1.2 in (3 cm) across

▲ Hydrocotyle sibthorpiodes *is found above water in the wild.*

▶ *Continual pruning of* Hydrocotyle verticillata *will create dense growth.*

Floating plants

Floating plants perform several useful roles in the aquarium. Primarily, they add a touch of real life to the display, echoing the plant-strewn surface waters of rivers and lakes in the wild. They also provide welcome shade for other plants and cover for surface-dwelling fishes. Floating plants establish readily in the aquarium and will flourish in a well-lit environment.

◀ ▼ *Usually sold as a pond plant,* Eichhornia crassipes *can be kept in an open-top aquarium with reasonably bright lighting.*

* Some floating plants have well-developed buoyancy aids, such as swollen leaf bases.

◀ *In good conditions,* Azolla caroliniana *spreads rapidly and may need regular thinning.*

▶ ▼ *The thick, waxy leaves of* Limnobium laevigatum *are 0.8–1.2 in (2–3 cm) long. This adaptable floating plant may be kept in open-topped aquariums with adequate ventilation. It can spread rapidly.*

Trailing roots take up nutrients.

The leaves are almost round.

* Keep floating plants in check to prevent them from covering the entire surface of the aquarium.

Leaves grow on a horizontally growing stem.

▶ Ludwigia helminthorrhiza *does well in bright conditions. If planted in the substrate, it soon reaches the water surface.*

FLOATING PLANTS

Floating plants

Most floating plants have fine roots that absorb nutrients directly from the water and sustain the rapidly growing foliage. Fish welcome the protection these roots provide and also use them as breeding sites for their eggs. Floating plants with substantial leaves held above the surface thrive best in open-topped aquariums with suspended lights, which cannot scorch the foliage.

▼ *Small fish appreciate the shade provided by* Pistia stratiotes.

* *Still water is ideal for the smaller floating plants. They will suffer in the strong currents from filters.*

POND OR AQUARIUM?

Many floating plants suitable for the aquarium will also prosper in a garden pond, although some will die down in the colder months. In the aquarium, they enjoy cooler conditions than plants found in tropical regions. Check plant labels for ideal temperature ranges.

▲ *Provide adequate ventilation for* Salvinia auriculata *above the water surface.*

FLOATING PLANTS

◀ *Liquid fertilization and good lighting will ensure that* Salvinia natans *grows strongly.*

Finely feathered roots are clearly visible.

Propagate Riccia by division.

▲ Riccia fluitans *produces a dense clump of separate plants that float on the water surface.*

◀ *The leaves of* Salvinia oblongifolia *are more extended and elongate than in other* Salvinia *species.*

Picture credits

Additional picture credits

The publishers would like to thank the
following photographers for providing the
images credited here by page number
and position: T(Top), B(Bottom), C(Center),
BL(Bottom Left), etc.

David Allison: 18(BR)
Aqua Press (M-P & C Piednoir): 30(C), 43(T)
Jan-Eric Larsson: 7(TR)
Mike Sandford: 43(B)
William Tomey: 8 (BL)
Tropica (Ole Pedersen): 10(TL), 25(TL)